Looking Back
— AT —
South Shore
H I S T O R Y

From Plymouth Rock to Quincy Granite

John J. Galluzzo

Charleston · London

THE
History
PRESS

Published by The History Press
Charleston, SC 29403
www.historypress.net

Front cover, top: Scituate Lighthouse. *Photo by Jeremy D'Entremont
(www.newenglandlighthouses.net).*

First published 2013

Manufactured in the United States

ISBN 978.1.60949.723.1

Library of Congress CIP data applied for.

Contents

CONTENTS

Acknowledgements

Where do I begin? I guess at the top. I'd like to thank Maria Ferri and the staff at *South Shore Living* and Rabideau Publishing for the wonderful opportunities I've had to explore our region's history for the past decade or so. I'd like to thank Maria's predecessor, Jaci Conry, for the same.

I'd also like to thank my South Shore coauthors: David Ball, Fred Freitas, Carol Miles and David Corbin in Scituate; Cynthia Hagar Krusell in Marshfield; and Don Cann in Rockland, Abington, the Isles of Shoals, Camp Edwards...well, we've been everywhere together.

The following people have been helpful to me in preparing these articles, some many years ago: Alden Ringquist of Project Gurnet and Big Lights; Bob Gallagher, keeper of Scituate Light; Donna Curtin of the Plymouth Antiquarian Society; Marilyn Kozodoy of the Isaac Sprague Appreciation Society; the entire staff of Stellwagen Bank National Marine Sanctuary, from top to bottom; photographer Bob Michelson; Tim Davidson and the volunteers of the Marshfield Historical Society; Wayne Petersen, David Ludlow and others from Mass Audubon, and David Clapp, formerly thereof; Patrick Browne and the staff and volunteers of the Duxbury Rural and Historical Society; Jack Spurr and Kerri Spurr Gallaway of A.W. Perry, Inc.; Norman Tucker and all my friends at the Jones River Village Historical Society in Kingston; sports historian John Liffman; Carrie Anne Wolverton; Suzanne Buchanan and the volunteers of the Hingham Historical Society; Debbie Wall, Karen Proctor and the historians of Pembroke; Ed Fitzgerald, Dan Johnson and the volunteers of the Quincy Historical Society; Susan

Acknowledgements

Ovans and Roger Jackson of the *Hull Times*, who took my "stuff" and ran with it long before I got to *South Shore Living*; Jim and Peggy Baker of Plymouth; David Hickey of Whitman; and Peter Arenstam and the crew of *Mayflower II*. And then there are the history rovers who may not have particularly aided me in the development of these stories but have always been there to bounce ideas off of: Judeth Van Hamm, Al Almeida, Kathy O'Malley, Rick Shaner, Doug Bingham, Dr. Bill Thiesen of the U.S. Coast Guard, Mark Schmidt and Fred Morin. Bob and Greg Lessard will be thanked in future books, as I foresee great things coming from the three of us.

Chris Haraden is one of my oldest friends. I envision us still calling each other in our eighties trying to figure out what our next big projects should be.

Mostly, I'd like to thank Richard Cleverly of Hull, who indulged and encouraged my history cravings as a young man. It's mostly because of him that I love my hometown and the towns that surround it.

And, of course, there's Michelle and the boys, Ben and Anthony. Any errors in this book are mine; any royalties that come from it will be theirs, I'm sure.

Introduction

I'm not sure, but I think I pulled one over on Maria Ferri, the editor at *South Shore Living*. I'll never forget the day she called me and asked me if I had a plan for the upcoming year of "Look Back" articles.

Year? I thought.

To that point, I had been a somewhat regular contributor to the column, but by no means did I consider myself the owner of it. By no means was it "mine." But thinking quickly, I said, "Oh, of course I have. I can send you a list of suggestions by e-mail this afternoon." I had no idea what would be on that list.

But that wasn't a problem. By that time, I had authored a couple of dozen books on local history and worked with many of the wonderful historians that dedicate themselves to telling the stories of the small towns of the South Shore. I was constantly keeping up with upcoming local anniversaries—centennials, sesquicentennials, tercentennials, etc.—no matter how big or small. Over the years, that would become my favorite annual tradition: looking ahead to the past.

I forwarded Maria a list, and we went to work. So far, so good. Right, Maria?

She's given me some autonomy over the years, allowing me to come up with the bones of the schedule, but I've always reached out to her for her approval, her ideas and, if necessary, her astutely thought out rejections. I've done my best to find historic tales that stick to the monthly themes of the magazine, and once in a while, I've been lucky enough to write a feature to which I can link the "Look Back," giving the magazine that little bit of consistency from page to page.

No story is out of bounds. I've written about the Pilgrims, and I've covered Hurricane Bob (it *was* more than twenty years ago, after all). I've tried to make sure that I've touched all the communities in the region, but some towns I've certainly covered more than others. I take each year as a challenge. Sometimes I throw together a list that purposely has four or five stories on it of which I know very little, other than the fact they happened on the South Shore. I force myself into the libraries and museums, to speak to the historians, the librarians, the curators, the people who know their local history best. Every once in a while, I find something that no one has touched for years, decades, even a century. I make connections that perhaps have not been made before, playing the "What If?" game that historians so love. And I take every opportunity I can to hype the events of our local historical societies, our nature conservancies, our hometowns, to help people better understand our common past. The "Look Back" stories, I hope, help to define the character of the South Shore.

And I'd be lying if I said that I wasn't having fun.

The South Shore is one of the birthplaces of the United States, and I've always maintained that one thing that makes it special is that it has quantitatively more history than most other regions of the country. But it also has good, quality history. The first American lighthouse? Off Hull. The first man to fly a navy plane across the Atlantic? From Hanson. The first man to throw a pitch at Fenway Park? From Brockton. Abraham Lincoln's ancestral line ran right through Hull, Cohasset, Hingham and Scituate. The man who accepted the sword of surrender from Lord Cornwallis at Yorktown to end the Revolutionary War was from Hingham. The inventor of the Toll House Cookie ran her empire in Whitman. More on her later.

There is no shortage of ideas for the future. 2014? Bicentennial of Scituate Lighthouse's "Army of Two" story, 100th anniversary of the opening of the Cape Cod Canal, 50th anniversary of the last major wildfire in Myles Standish State Forest. 2016? Tercentennial of Boston Lighthouse, centennial of the founding of the Scituate Historical Society. 2020? Hmm, what happened around here in 1620?

The beauty of writing the "Look Back" article each month is manifested in the smiles I see on the faces of people who come up to me and say, "That was fantastic what you wrote this month in *South Shore Living!*" even if I have no idea what article they just read. I just nod my head and say, "You wouldn't believe how much fun I had writing it!" Then, I really hope they come back with, "You know what? I've got a topic for you. My great-great uncle, back in 1926, was living in Ah-de-nah…." Each story I learn, each new historical

Introduction

South Shore character I meet, enriches my life, and I hope it does the same for every reader of my column when that person's story comes around.

There it is—I said "my column." After all these years, I guess I feel like it's my own child, which makes sense. The towns of the South Shore have always been my home, and my historian friends are my extended family.

Enjoy the stories in this book, some of my favorite articles from *South Shore Living* from the past decade. And if they spark a familiar thought in your mind, share it with me. I want to know your South Shore history.

1724: The House that Jumped

Although its foundation is shaky, the story of the home of Elijah Cushing of Hanson, if it proves to be true, may be one of the most telling tales of life in the early days of the South Shore of Massachusetts.

Elijah was a Scituate man, and he married a Scituate woman. Elizabeth "Debbie" Barstow had already been married once, to Isaac Barker in 1720, but for some reason, that marriage failed; perhaps, and most likely, on Isaac's death. Elijah and Debbie married on January 7, 1725, and nine months later—almost to the day—Elijah Jr. was born.

Local legend holds that Elijah the elder built a house in 1724 at the corner of Liberty and Washington Streets in what was then Abington. "Strong oak timbers cut and trimmed in the nearby forest went into the frame," wrote historian Bertha H. Baresel in 1962. "Between the inside and outside finish there is a solid brick wall, so that today the house stands as true as when erected, so long ago. Inside, fine paneling and the fireplaces please the eye." Although Elijah Jr.'s birth is listed as having taken place in Hanover in 1725, there *was* no Hanover in 1725. It would incorporate two years later from the western part of Scituate and the eastern part of Abington, to the dismay of Abingtonians, who felt that they were losing both land and resources in the deal they could never recover. Elijah was one of the eight men who signed the petition for the formation of the new town. Hanover, possibly named for the Hanoverian kings of England, became the thirteenth town in Plymouth County in 1727.

And at that point, Elijah Cushing's house jumped from one town to the next, without moving an inch. But wait, there's more.

Elijah Cushing's house still stands today, nearly three centuries after it was built and in its fourth different town.

In 1746, Elijah Cushing's little area of Hanover was suffering an identity crisis. He certainly wasn't. In the intervening years, he had served as deacon of the First Congregational Church, as a justice of the peace, the town's first representative to the General Court and as selectman from 1728 to 1739. In that latter year, serving as a lieutenant colonel of the militia, he mustered in local boys for a pending invasion of Canada. As early as 1740, his home served as a gathering place for men from Pembroke and beyond who were unhappy with Great Britain's increasingly tyrannical rule. In 1744, as a captain, he was given control of the town's munitions. With its master's personal prominence, "the house was a social center for miles around, Mr. Cushing being representative to the General Court and selectman, with a family of three popular daughters and two sons, with many slaves to carry on, and he entertained lavishly. There were gay house parties and other joyful occasions."

But things were not quite right. As early as 1746, efforts were underway to set off the western portion of the town of Pembroke as its own community and to take with it parts of Hanover, Abington, Bridgewater and Halifax. Eight years later, the ruling came down. "Saturday, 8th of June, 1754," reads the old colonial record, "on petition of Elijah Cushing, esq., agent for the second precinct in Pembroke, showing that said precinct is made up of four several towns besides Pembroke, and praying that the whole Precinct may be united to Pembroke, the General Court ordered that the Petitioners with their estates comprehended within the bounds of said Precinct be to all intents and purposes annex to and made part of the Town of Pembroke."

Without moving an inch, Elijah Cushing's house moved into its third South Shore town.

But wait, there's more.

Just two years later, twenty-three-year-old Benjamin Lincoln of Hingham, an aspiring military man, would wait patiently for Mary, Elijah and Debbie's eldest daughter, to decide on an answer to his question. Yes, she would marry him, in Pembroke on January 15, 1756. Lincoln would go onto a distinguished career as both a public servant and a warrior, standing in as General George Washington's surrogate at Yorktown in 1781 to accept the British sword of surrender that signified the triumphant end of the American Revolution. Elijah, though, never saw the day, having passed away in 1762.

His house, though, remained, and was passed down through the generations. It was still standing in 1819, when yet another agitation arose for the West Parish of Pembroke to be split off as its own community. On May 26 of that year, a petition was presented to the General Court. Finally, on February 22, 1820, the wish was granted: Hanson was born. The community took for its name the surname of A.C. Hanson, the "Father of the Free Press" and a martyr of the tumultuous days of the War of 1812.

And with that, Elijah Cushing's house jumped to its fourth town, without moving an inch. And it's still standing today.

1773: A Tale of Two Thomases

The first John Thomas to reach America did so as a young man of thirteen or fourteen years of age, arriving from his birthplace of Modbury, Devon, England, on September 11, 1635, aboard the *Hopewell*. Orphaned and destitute, the youngster arrived in Marshfield and survived only through the generosity of that town's first citizen. "He was taken into the family of Gov. Winslow, Green Harbor," wrote historian Lysander Richards in his *History of Marshfield*, "and became steward of the estate."

John did well in his new home, marrying Sarah Pitney on December 21, 1648, only the third marriage recorded in the history of the community. Together, they raised eight children, including a son named Samuel, born in 1652. Samuel and his wife, Mercy Ford, had ten kids, including Nathan, born in 1688, and John, born in 1690. John had a son named John, born in 1724, and Nathan had a son named Ichabod, born in 1733. Those youngsters, separated by nine years of age and just the distance from Green Harbor to Brant Rock, would each have a significant impact on a war a half a century into the future.

The youngest John Thomas studied medicine as a young man under Cotton Tufts in Medford, beginning a long military career in 1746 at the age of twenty-one. He rose through the ranks, first as a medical officer and then as a combat officer, leading a regiment in Nova Scotia during the French and Indian War. When that conflict ended, he moved to Kingston with his wife, Hannah (whose maiden name was also Thomas). John Thomas served his new hometown well, as selectman from 1763 to 1775 and as town clerk. In

The history of Gurnet Lighthouse begins with the Thomas family. *Courtesy of the author.*

February 1768, he agreed to allow the colonial legislature to construct twin lighthouses on his land at the Gurnet, on the bluff at the southern end of Duxbury Beach. In September, with the legislature paying him rent for the land, he became the first keeper of the Gurnet Lighthouses.

When the American Revolution broke out, John left Hannah to tend the lights, making her the first female lighthouse keeper in America. On February 9, 1775, the Provincial Congress created the post of lieutenant general, appointing Thomas to the position. On March 4, 1776, Lieutenant General John Thomas led a troop of 2,500 men from Roxbury to Dorchester Heights, forcing the evacuation of the British soldiers stationed there thirteen days later, an event still celebrated in Boston every year. Appointed major general on March 6, Thomas accepted an assignment in Canada but died of smallpox on June 2, 1776, at fifty-two years old.

Meanwhile, cousin Ichabod Thomas led a relatively less exciting life. On January 22, 1761, Ichabod married Ruth Turner of Pembroke. Ruth's father, Captain Benjamin Turner, had arrived at the "Brick Kilns" on the North River in 1730 and begun building ships. He passed his knowledge on to his son-in-law Ichabod in at least two ways. In 1765, the young man built his first ship, the brig *Norfolk*, and that same year, Governor Francis Bernard appointed him captain of a troop of horses, the same position held by his father-in-law.

Ichabod's career would be spent primarily at the Pembroke shipyard on the North River, starting a family (Ichabod Jr. was born nine months and one day after his parents' wedding) and constructing sailing ships. The *Neptune* followed the *Norfolk*, and the *Lima* followed the *Neptune*. Early in the 1770s, Ichabod launched a brig that fought its way out of the river to sea under the name *Beaver*.

On October 18, 1773, Ichabod's *Beaver* left London in convoy with six other ships—the *London*, headed for Charleston; the *Polly*, headed for Philadelphia; the *Nancy*, for New York; and the *Eleanor*, *Dartmouth* and *William*, which were joining the *Beaver* on the way to Boston—and sailed across the Atlantic.

The *Dartmouth* arrived in Boston Harbor on November 27, the *Eleanor* sailed into port on December 2 and the *Beaver* arrived off Rainsford Island on December 7—with one small problem: it was carrying smallpox. Quarantined for a week, the brig underwent a cleansing process and was then freed to join the others at Griffin's Wharf in the city on December 15. News reached the city that the *William* had wrecked on Cape Cod, a total loss.

The incident that followed has become a staple event in history textbooks for American schoolchildren for decades. Certain residents of

Boston, outraged by the imposition of taxes on goods imported into the colonies under the Townshend Act of 1767—specifically on glass, paper, lead, painter's colors and tea—stormed the three ships on Thursday night, December 16, 1773, and took their contents, ninety thousand pounds of the British East India Company's tea, and dumped it all in the ocean. Ichabod Thomas's brig *Beaver* had become an unwitting guest to the Boston Tea Party. The act fell into queue as one of the causes of the American Revolution, the conflict that would take the life of Ichabod's cousin John.

Had Ichabod never built the *Beaver*, would John have died when he did? Would Hannah Thomas have become the first female lighthouse keeper in American history? We will never know.

1811: The First Keeper of Scituate Lighthouse

The Massachusetts coast was a dark place two centuries ago. Boston Light had been lit for the first time in 1716 but did not survive the American Revolution. The governing body that emerged from the war, that new nation formed on the strength of its belief in every man's right to life, liberty and the pursuit of happiness, rebuilt it in 1783. Gurnet Light was lit in 1768, and out on Cape Cod, at the urging of the Boston Marine Society, a gathering of sea captains and merchants dedicated to improving the navigational framework of Boston Harbor and its approaches, the new government built Highland Light at Truro in 1797. For another fourteen years, that was it.

In 1811, though, rumors began of the pending construction of a second lighthouse on the South Shore. Secretary of the Treasury Albert Gallatin confirmed those rumors with a letter to Henry Dearborn, superintendent of lighthouses in Massachusetts, on March 27 of that year: "Sir, I have received your letter of the 8th inst. and enclose herewith proposals for building a light house, etc., at the entrance to Scituate Harbor, which you will cause to be published in one of the papers printed at Boston." The bidding war would begin, with Dearborn tasked with assessing the "stability of the persons" submitting offers to take on the task of building the new lighthouse.

Once rumors of a lighthouse began, so, too, did the rush to get the federally appointed position of the first Scituate Lighthouse keeper. In mid-April, Captain Andrew Churchill of Plympton hand-delivered a letter to Dearborn from a supporter, Henry Warren, recommending Churchill "as a

Scituate Light was about fifteen feet shorter during the Bates family's time than it is today. *Courtesy of Scituate Historical Society.*

suitable person to keep the light house at Scituate. I have not the pleasure of personal knowledge of him," Warren continued, noting, though, that people of whom he thought very highly thought very highly of Churchill. Churchill followed up with a letter of his own a week later. Referring to a rumor that the name of Scituate's Simeon Bates had been forwarded to Henry Dearborn as the man for the job, he wrote, "Bates is master of a vessel…has a home…which if I had the same I think that I should not wish to take the light house from him if he was in my position." Playing the underdog role, perhaps begging for a bit of charity, Churchill made his pitch.

Another dog would enter the fight, though, a few weeks later, when a letter signed by more than two dozen prominent Scituate and Hingham citizens made its way to Dearborn's desk calling for the ascension of Cornelius Bates

The Scituate Historical Society recently celebrated the bicentennial of Scituate Lighthouse. *Courtesy of the author.*

to the position of keeper. "We, the subscribers, being acquainted with the above Cornelius Bates, do approve of his being appointed keeper of the lighthouse about to be built at Scituate Harbor. He is a man of sobriety, industry and economy." Among the names on the list were Ebenezer Bailey, the town clerk, and Israel Litchfield, the West End storeowner for whom "Itchy's Corner" is still named today.

Through July and August, more letters flew in supporting Churchill, including one from Scituate Harbor sea captain Seth Sprague. On September 12, though, the picture got even murkier. Jesse Dunbar of Scituate took it upon himself to note that the men who signed the Cornelius Bates petition "live remote from this part of the town," meaning the harbor village, an apparent affront to the sea captains who would be depending upon the light for safety when entering the harbor. Furthermore, he said, "Captain Simeon Bates, a seafaring man, will if necessary obtain double the signatures and as respectable at least as the others."

Finally, in October, while the light was well near completion, a fourth man—and the third one with the surname Bates—sent in an application for the keeper's job. Josiah Bates found yet another angle from which to attack the problem. He wrote:

> *During the Revolutionary War, I was a soldier, a part of the time in the regiment of General* [then Colonel] *Knox and in other regiments during the whole war. Since that time, I have been employed at different times as Pilot of Armed Vessels belonging to the U.S. and am now employed in the Marine Hospital. Under such circumstances from your well-known patriotism, willingness to assist those who have been Servants of their Country, I have been induced to believe that you would render me any service consistent with the good of our country in your power.*

The Boston Marine Society asked for a delay in the lighting of the lamp on October 23, targeting April 1, 1812, as the society wanted to be assured of a proper "distinguishing mark" for the lighthouse.

In the end, on December 12, the job went to Simeon Bates, oddly the one man from whom we have no surviving letter of application for the position. Because of his acceptance of the job, we now have the story of the "American Army of Two," in which his daughters chased away the British navy with a fife and a drum during the War of 1812.

But that is a story for another day.

1813: *Chesapeake* vs. *Shannon*

The War of 1812 had come as a frustration to the people of the South Shore. Ancient hatreds still lingered against the British, for the Revolution had ended just three decades earlier. Yet here they were again, harassing the coastline, blockading Boston Harbor and the smaller ports of Cape Cod Bay, capturing merchant ships, impressing American sailors into Royal Navy duty.

Warfare at sea had never been a specialty of the new country. The rebelling colonies had relied on the French to provide firepower on the ocean, to essentially be the American navy, during the Revolution. The Revenue Cutter Service, a predecessor agency of today's Coast Guard, had launched its first "cutter" in 1791, the *Massachusetts*, from a Newburyport shipyard. By 1798, the country's navy had grown to about twenty-five vessels, including the USS *Constellation* and the USS *Constitution*. In early one-on-one engagements during the War of 1812, U.S. ships fared well against the British, but in total force, the United States Navy was no match for the Royal Navy.

Captain James Lawrence of the U.S. Navy took command of the USS *Chesapeake* in May 1813, intending to sail her out of Boston on the first good-weather day after her needed repairs were completed. As the month wore on, though, her end neared, in the guns of the HMS *Shannon*, patrolling the coast nearby. *Shannon*'s captain, Philip Broke, issued Lawrence a challenge:

> As the Chesapeake *appears now ready for sea, I request you will do me the favour to meet the* Shannon *with her, ship to ship, to try the*

The battle between the *Chesapeake* and *Shannon* could be seen, at least initially, from many vantage points on the South Shore. *Courtesy of the U.S. Navy.*

fortune of our respective flags. We have both noble motives. You will feel it as a compliment if I say that the result of our meeting may be the most grateful service I can render to my country; and I doubt not that you, equally confident of success, will feel convinced that it is only by repeated triumphs in even combats that your little navy can now hope to console your country for the loss of that trade it can no longer protect. Favour me with a speedy reply. We are short of provisions and water, and cannot stay long here.

Lawrence never received the note. Nevertheless, on June 1, 1813, *Chesapeake* sailed out of Boston Harbor and met HMS *Shannon* about twenty nautical miles east of Boston Light. *Chesapeake* made a show of its appearance, flying three American ensigns and a flag that read "Free Trade and Sailors' Rights," the root causes of the war on the American side.

As the *Chesapeake* headed for the scene of battle, Scituate and Cohasset residents crowded on the shoreline. Hingham residents climbed to the top of Turkey Hill, and Hull residents clambered to the crests of their northern prominences as well. Small boats set out from numerous nearby ports and followed close by to catch a glimpse of the action to come.

The result was almost a foregone conclusion. *Chesapeake*'s crew, although larger, was newer and untrained. *Shannon*'s crew, depleted by the necessity of sending off small numbers of men with each prize vessel the ship had captured, was nonetheless battle-tested and relentlessly drilled by the inventive Broke.

The ships squared off at 5:30 p.m., but the first shots were not fired until just before 6:00, from a distance of thirty-five meters. As they closed in on one another, the *Chesapeake* fared the worse. Both captains signaled for their crews to board the other ships, but the American bugler nervously fumbled the call, and the British moved first. Lawrence, already suffering a leg wound, took a bullet in the stomach that would prove fatal.

From shore, the scene became blurred. The smoke from the ships' guns obscured the battle, leaving the South Shore residents bewildered as to what was truly happening.

Knowing their captain was not long to live, the Americans hauled him below to the ship's surgeon. With a last gasp exhortation to his men, Lawrence shouted words that would live long as a motto of the United States Navy: "Don't give up the ship!" Alas, his command could not be heeded that day. The Americans fought bravely, even wounding Broke as he boarded the ship, but in the end—after just ten or eleven minutes of combat—both the day and the *Chesapeake* belonged to the British.

The people of the South Shore knew the result for certain when they watched *Shannon* hauling away *Chesapeake* as a prize. They had watched one of the most important naval battles in the history of the young country.

1815: The Untrue Life of Lucy Brewer

Through a series of ill-timed and ill-designed embargoes, President Thomas Jefferson caused a dockside traffic jam in the northeast in the years leading up to the War of 1812. With heavy duties inflicted on ships entering U.S. ports and restrictions on American ships trading in foreign ports, both at a time when British warships were actively expanding their ranks by impressing American sailors into the Royal Navy, the first decade of the nineteenth century was no time to be a seagoing merchant. As such, port towns like Plymouth suffered.

In 1809, the town voted "to petition the state legislators, that they devise and pursue such measures as their judgment shall dictate, to relieve the people from the severe pressure under which they are suffering from the embargo laws." No haranguing toward that end, though, would stop the approach of war. In July 1812, the town voted to "protest against an alliance with despotic France, whose friendship, more than its enmity, has been fatal to every other republic on the globe" and hopefully avoid an "impending war, particularly distressing and ruinous to this section of our country." In short, according to James Thacher in his *History of Plymouth*, "The town was unanimous for peace and not for war."

War came, though, to Plymouth. British warships cruised the coast, blockading Massachusetts ports, though from time to time, a privateer worked its way out. Plymouth men sailed on ships from Boston and worked as some of the most effective disrupters of British shipping the young nation had. With constant threat of attack from the enemy, Duxbury, Kingston and Plymouth coordinated defense of the harbor. Night watches roamed the streets. After a request to the governor for a military presence, Colonel Caleb Howard and a regiment of militia settled in town, "which gave the place the aspect of a garrison town, for several months," noted Thacher.

After the war, an even more interesting tale of Plymouth was woven.

In a pamphlet written in 1815, a young woman named Louisa Baker claimed that she grew up on a farm near Plymouth, but due to an unwanted pregnancy and her partner's reluctance to marry her, she fled to Boston to avoid the surely forthcoming shame. She was duped into working in a brothel and then, after the baby died in childbirth, took the Deborah Sampson route—she disguised herself as a man named George Baker and joined the crew of the USS *Constitution*, with whom she sailed for three years undetected. Two other cross-dressing tales followed, including one in which she disguised herself as a man and defended a woman's honor by challenging her bully to a duel. The pamphlets, eventually published in book form as *The Female Marine, or The Adventures of Lucy Brewer*, published by Nathaniel Coverly, became a raging success. Nineteen editions were published between 1815 and 1818.

Sadly, the story never happened. While genealogical research may not have every answer, the fact is that the facts don't stand up. No woman named Lucy Brewer existed in the Plymouth area at that time, nor did a Louisa Baker, nor an Eliza Bowen, a third name later used in connection with the story. There is no trace of her husband, George West, whom she marries and with whom she eventually settles down.

Instead, the stories are most likely fictitious collected works of the publisher, Coverly, and possibly his "hack" writer, Nathaniel Hill Wright. The accounts of life on the *Constitution* are taken almost verbatim from newspaper reports of the day, provided by the captain himself.

But true or not, Lucy Brewer has a moral tale to tell. While providing readers the angles of romance and loss, of adventure and valor, *The Female Marine* expands to give warning to young men. The book's stated intended audience of "sailors, prostitutes and juveniles" read stern advice against visiting certain parts of the city of Boston where prostitution openly existed. A diversionary tale in the second part of the book laments the death of a seventeen-year-old boy who fell in love with a prostitute at the brothel in which Lucy worked and then succumbed to a sexually transmitted disease. In 1822, Mayor Josiah Quincy of Boston led America's first major war against the practice of the oldest profession.

Lucy's tale falls in line with others in the genre at the time, including British author Robert Kirby's tales of Mary Anne Talbot, who fictitiously served her country in the Napoleonic Wars. What both Brewer and Talbot did was inspire continued patriotism—and line the pockets of their mysterious but crafty creators in the early days of the nineteenth century.

1843: Up the Missouri with John James Audubon

The topic of "great botanical artists of the nineteenth century" is not one that routinely comes up for discussion at South Shore dinner parties. But were the South Shore population at large to know more about Isaac Sprague, perhaps somewhere, sometime each spring, someone would take a sip of chardonnay, glance at a fellow reveler and causally say, "So, did you know that John James Audubon once picked a guy from Hingham to be his personal artist on a trip up the Missouri River? No, really—it's true."

OK, it's a far-fetched scenario. But the story is true.

Isaac Sprague was born on Pleasant Street in Hingham on September 5, 1811. As a youngster, he showed artistic talent, which was encouraged by his mother. "I always had a fondness for making pictures, and I made small drawings when at school, using a black lead pencil," he said. His father, "a quiet intellectual man, a cooper by trade," according to Miss Ellen Lincoln, speaking before the Hingham Agassiz Chapter in May 1888, felt, though, that artists were "invariably poor." When Isaac's father died in 1825, the young man apprenticed with his Uncle Blossom, putting his artistic talents to use as a carriage painter.

But the restraints of the workaday world could not hold him. Possibly encouraged by his brother Hosea, an employee of the Boston Athenaeum, Isaac took to nature exploration and drawing. His sharp acuity, which would be his hallmark, showed at a young age. According to Lincoln, "Where an ordinary observer would discern only an ordinary whortleberry bush, he could see the berries also." In 1836, he became particularly fascinated with the study of birds after receiving a copy of Thomas Nuttall's 1832 *A Manual of the Ornithology of the United States and Canada*. He sought every species he could for study and drawing, preferring to sketch live specimens, but shooting others, which was customary at the time, when needed. His renderings, beginning with his first, a "chewink" (more commonly known today as an Eastern Towhee), soon drew attention from some of the greatest names in the study of natural history in the United States.

In 1840, George Emerson, then preceptor at Hingham's Derby Academy, related to a distinguished guest, John James Audubon, the startling accuracy of Sprague's work. Upon seeing some drawings, Audubon was impressed enough to ask the young man to join him on a trip up the Missouri River by steamboat to help him compile his upcoming work on the quadrupeds of North America. Single and ready for adventure, specifically the notion of following the footsteps of Nuttall and, perhaps more importantly, childhood heroes Meriwether Lewis and William Clark, Sprague accepted.

The Hingham artist left his name along the banks of the Missouri, thanks to his quiet perseverance in challenging the identification of a bird by Audubon. The Frenchman shot a specimen and declared it to be a specific type of lark in winter plumage; Sprague claimed it was something else, a species never identified by Audubon in his *Birds of America* series. Audubon scoffed. Nonplussed, Sprague patiently waited in the wilderness for another bird of the species to return to its nest. When it did, he shot it, gathered the bird, nest and eggs and presented them to Audubon, who admitted his mistake. He apologetically gave the bird its new scientific name: *Nevrorys Spraguii*, or "Sprague's Missouri Lark," today's Sprague's Pipit.

Sprague returned from his trip and found immediate work in the summer of 1844 on Nantasket Beach, helping to run the Beach House, an early boardinghouse. Within a year, his star began a second ascendancy. Harvard botanist Asa Gray discovered the still-young Sprague's talents and convinced him to move to Cambridge to be closer to the academic scene of the city. Sprague did so in June 1845, but not before taking another major step in life. A habitual diarist, Sprague recorded two—and only two—important words on December 10, 1844: "Married Hannah."

Sprague filled a much-needed role for Gray, that of an artist to illustrate his proposed works on the native plants of North America. Gray, the first noted American botanist, referred to Sprague as the "most accurate of living botanical artists," who, according to Dr. G. Edmund Gifford in the February 1975 *Massachusetts Audubon Newsletter*, "raised the level of botanical illustration in this country to that of the great European centers."

Sprague's concentration on flora led to a lifelong career in illustrating such works as Gray's 1856 *Manual of Botany*, William Oakes's *White Mountain Scenery*, Reverend A.B. Hervey's *Flowers of the Field and Forest* and George Lincoln Goodale's *Wild Flowers of North America*. His final published drawings graced the pages of Hervey's *Wayside Flowers and Ferns* in 1887. Sprague died at his home in Wellesley Hills on March 13, 1895, at eighty-three years old. According to Lincoln, "The father's fears, that the son would not attain wealth as an artist, were realized." Sprague died "not rich in dollars and cents" but with "compensation in the consciousness of a great work, well done, and a name and a fame world-renowned."

1851: "Won't Stand Over To-Nite"

The old-timers who remember it are now long gone, but there was a time when you could ask any South Shore resident about the worst storm that Mother Nature ever subjected them to, and he or she would undoubtedly answer, "Oh, I'll never forget the Minot's Light gale."

Although the storm had implications from New York to Maine and left various alterations that affected other South Shore communities (the spring on the ancient homestead of Myles Standish in Duxbury, for instance, dried up after the storm), it has been forever linked to the loss of the original Minot's Lighthouse, which once stood, shakily, off the coast of Scituate and Cohasset.

A catastrophic design flaw championed by engineer Captain William C. Swift of the U.S. Army Topographical Corps led to the ultimate doom of the original tower. Swift firmly believed that his design—a "rocket-shaped" lantern room atop nine legs driven into the rocky Minot Ledge, a style known as "screwpile" construction—would withstand storms better than a standard granite tower. Under his theory, the rushing water driven by storms would pass through the legs and expend the bulk of its energy elsewhere, rather than smashing against the walls of a granite structure. Keeper Isaac Dunham, who took on the duties of lightkeeper on January 1, 1850, immediately requested the tower be strengthened with cross braces, to no avail.

The storm that claimed the tower began on April 12 and raged for four days, forcing assistant lighthouse keepers Joseph Wilson and Joseph Antoine

(Dunham had resigned after just nine months, and the new keeper, John Bennett, had gone ashore for supplies before the storm) to subsist on dry bread and raw meat for its duration. Bennett had described the tower as shaking "like a drunken man" during high winds, and Wilson and Antoine confirmed that notion by dropping a note in a bottle into the water the night of the fatal gale that read, "The lighthouse won't stand over to-nite. She shakes two feet each way now."

What happened next is still a mystery to this day. Sometime around one o'clock in the morning on April 17, 1851, a loud gong and crash tore through the air off the Scituate and Cohasset coastlines, audible above the din of the storm. When the storm dissipated and the local residents stepped outside of their homes the next morning, the uninterrupted horizon to the east showed that Minot's Lighthouse was gone, presumably knocked into the sea by the storm.

Various theories exist as to how and why the tower came down. One states that a platform placed under the cabin for storage of oil barrels, and ostensibly to give the lightkeepers more living space, took a pounding from the waves below, thrusting the lighthouse upward and causing the iron legs to fail. A second theory poses the question of whether or not a mooring stone for a line stretching from the lantern room to the sea was moved by the wave action of the storm, dragging the lighthouse to its demise. Under this idea, one would need to determine the power needed to move the mooring stone and the tensile strength of the line attached to it.

No matter the cause, the most heartrending outcome of the incident was the loss of the two keepers, Wilson and Antoine. More than a century and a half later, the residents of the South Shore and even the Coast Guard found ways to remember the fallen men.

Cohasset's Government Island, in Cohasset Harbor, sports a replica of the current Minot's Lighthouse lantern room and the ground template on which the various courses of granite were laid out prior to construction of the new tower on Minot's Ledge. There with them, surrounded by a compass rose, is a polished granite marker dedicated to the lives of Wilson and Antoine, designed and built by Antoine descendants Herb Jason and John Small of Cohasset.

On April 16, 2001, the sesquicentennial anniversary of the tower's loss, the Scituate Historical Society chartered a cruise boat and sailed to Minot's Light to cast a wreath on the water in memory of Wilson and Antoine. Jason, Small and several other Antoine descendants did the honor.

Finally, in the summer of 2007, the U.S. Coast Guard, spurred on by the nonprofit Foundation for Coast Guard History, organized a training program for Coast Guard divers around the base of the current Minot's Lighthouse. Their goal was to use the old lighthouse search as disaster training, simulating the protocols for a shipwreck or an airplane accident over water. The foundation's goal was to lower a plaque on a five-thousand-pound stone to the seafloor from the deck of the buoy tender *Abbie Burgess* in memory of the keepers. With the words, "Keeper Antoine, Keeper Wilson, your sacrifices have not been forgotten, and they will not be forgotten. May you rest in peace," Chief Warrant Officer Paul Dilger, commanding officer of the tender, ordered the stone overboard.

Although those who remember the storm are now gone, the echoes of the Minot's Light Storm still resonate along the South Shore.

1851: Thoreau on the South Shore

To everybody he met, he was probably just another stranger passing through. When Henry David Thoreau walked through Hull, Cohasset and other South Shore towns in the middle of the nineteenth century, he was toiling in pre-fame anonymity, exploring the world within his reach, journaling as he went.

But to the residents of those small towns, a stranger passing through stuck out like a sore thumb. In 1851, when the great transcendentalist naturalist stood atop Telegraph Hill in Hull and sketched what was then known as Hog Island, the local population stood at about 250 souls who rarely ventured anywhere by land. Among the many fishermen, wreckers and lobstermen, a man presenting himself as a writer by profession would have turned a head or two. Yet no Hull resident at that time could have known of the notoriety the odd, opinionated man would gain a century after he died.

Yet it's because of the wandering Thoreau, who once stated that he could see no reason to travel extensively as his own Concord was, to him, the most "estimable" place on earth, that we have some of the most interesting accounts of South Shore life in the 1850s. The first place to look is his posthumously published book, *Cape Cod*. For deeper insights, his raw journals provide even greater details.

On Friday, July 25, 1851, Thoreau walked through Hull on a hot day. "As I walked on the beach [Nantasket], panting with thirst, a man pointed to a white spot on the side of a distant hill (Strawberry Hill he called it) which rose from the gravelly beach, and said that there was a pure and cold

When not visiting Henry David Thoreau's South Shore haunts, historical interpreter Richard Smith can often be found in Thoreau's reconstructed cabin at Walden Pond. *Courtesy of the author.*

and unfailing spring." Until the iconic water tower was removed in 2009, Strawberry Hill continued its association with fresh, clean drinking water, yet Thoreau's description gives that history a layer many modern residents might not have known existed.

Later that day, in Cohasset, Thoreau noted the effects of a recent gale:

> *I saw in Cohasset, separated from the sea only by a narrow beach, a very large and handsome but shallow lake, of at least five rocky islets in it; which the sea had tossed over the beach in the great storm in the spring, and, after the alewives had passed into it, stopped up its outlet; and now the alewives were dying by the thousands, and the inhabitants apprehended a pestilence as the water evaporated.*

In 1849, Thoreau visited the Cohasset shore in time to catch sight of the wreck of the brig *St. John*. In 1851, he walked there just three months after the loss of the first Minot's Ledge Lighthouse.

In Scituate, he marveled at the stately beauty of the meetinghouses, perched upon the high grounds of the town. In Marshfield, he could not bite his tongue—or stay his pen, as it were—when viewing the lands of his spiritual enemy on the issue of slavery, Daniel Webster. He recorded secondhand stories of Webster's impatience with neighbors.

Thoreau visited Powder Point in Duxbury before there was a bridge to the beach. He gazed upon the mouth of the Eel River a century prior to the creation of Plimoth Plantation. And he recorded tales told by locals "of such places in Plymouth as 'Small Gains' and 'Shall I Go Naked?'"

With four hundred years of European settlement now in the rearview mirror of history on the South Shore, the trove of locally recorded historical material is certainly precious. But there can be no denying the power of the thoughts of an outsider, especially when that stranger was someone as talented and verbose as Henry David Thoreau.

1853: Daniel Webster and the Sea Serpent

It was a hard thing to come to grips with, but Daniel Webster was a man who never dodged the truth.

The story was told two ways. First, there was the *Personal Memorials of Daniel Webster, including A Sketch of his Public Life and the Particulars of his Death*, published in 1853. In this work, the author flowingly described the bond between Webster and his friend Seth Peterson, "a sometime farmer and sometime fisherman on the coast of Massachusetts," in Webster's own words. The two shared many a local adventure during a quarter-century of companionship, including that fateful day returning from an outing to Manomet when the famed Massachusetts sea serpent roared into their lives. The author wrote:

> *Those who are in doubt as to the existence of the great sea-serpent may be pleased to know that the testimony of both Mr. Webster and his skipper is on the side of the affirmative of this question. They both allege that they once saw some living animal answering to the popular description of this creature, and Mr. Webster asserts that a drawing taken of a specimen in Plymouth Bay was pronounced by the naturalists of Boston as exactly corresponding with an animal found on the coast of Norway, near the great whirlpool, and delineated by Tompoppidam in his history of Norway.*

Henry David Thoreau took the tale one step further. A decided opponent, perhaps a spiritual enemy of Webster, stemming from Webster's stand in support of the Compromise of 1850 (which allowed for new "slave states" to enter the United States, a concession Webster hoped would preserve the Union and avert a civil war), Thoreau delighted in exposing Webster's sighting. He wrote about it in his June 14, 1857 journal entry while on a visit to Clark's Island: "It passed directly across their bows only 6 or 7 rods off and then disappeared. On the sail, however, Webster having had time to reflect on what occurred, at length said to Peterson, 'For God's sake, never say a word about this to anyone—for if it should be known that I have seen the sea-serpent, I should never hear the last of it—but wherever I went I should have to tell the story to everyone I met.' So it has not leaked out," added Thoreau gleefully, "till now."

Daniel Webster, Marshfield's great orator and statesman, had a secret.

Sea serpent sightings had plagued Massachusetts for most of the nineteenth century, Gloucester being the center of the frenzy. The Linnaean Society of New England went as far as classifying the Gloucester serpent *Scoliophus atlanticus*, although that was later retracted. The answer as to what Webster and Peterson saw, though, may lie in one particular reference: Norway.

Bishop Erik Pontoppidan—not Tompoppidam, as corrupted in Webster's memorial—penned a fantastic description of a sea monster, the Kraken, in his 1755 *Natural History of Norway* but was also one of the first to depict a species of shark that still feeds in Plymouth Bay today, *Halsydrus maximus*. This shark, which reaches forty-five feet in length, filter feeds for plankton at the surface with a huge, gaping maw. When it reaches its maximum size, its dorsal fin loses the ability to support itself out of the water and flops over. The effect is one of a giant open-mouthed snake swishing through the water.

When the shark dies, it decomposes in such a way that its gill apparatus falls away, leaving a small head and neck separated from the bulk of the body. Pectoral and pelvic fins can remain, but tattered looking, they can call to mind small legs, giving the carcass a prehistoric, plesiosaur-like profile.

Through the years, the classification of *Halsydrus maximus* has changed at least seventeen times, including *Halsydrus pontoppidani* in 1809, in honor of the Bishop of Bergen, and *Scoliophus atlanticus* in 1817. In 1842, it gained the name *Squalus rhinoceros*, in reference to its bulbous nose-like protuberance, and a century later gained the name by which scientists know it today: *Cetorhinus maximus*, the basking shark.

Did Daniel Webster see a sea monster? If indeed he saw a basking shark, the answer is no, unless you're a phytoplankton. Basking sharks, while ferocious looking, are among the most gentle creatures in the sea, and their slow-moving surface-feeding technique has led to their global decline, as they are hunted for food, bait and even for an aphrodisiac. If Daniel Webster saw a basking shark, he saw one of the world's most stirring natural sights—but no monster.

1854: Henry Stellwagen's Bank

About halfway through the nineteenth century, the U.S. Coast Survey borrowed an officer from the U.S. Navy, sending him to Massachusetts waters to determine new sites for federally financed lifeboats. That officer, Lieutenant Henry Stellwagen, wrote the following to U.S. Coast Survey Superintendent Alexander Dallas Bache on November 12, 1853, from Philadelphia:

> *Sir: I have received your letter of the 9ᵗʰ instant and respectfully submit the following report concerning the location of life-boats on the coast of Massachusetts.*
>
> *I visited, according to your instructions, the light-house stations at Nausett and Cohasett, and at each place found that boats had already been placed by the Massachusetts Humane Society, and subsequently learned officially from R.B. Forbes, Esq., and other officers of that society, that some forty or forty-one boats are stationed at intervals along the coast of the State, occupying nearly every suitable and required spot.*

Stellwagen, not easily convinced, opted to take the grand tour of the Massachusetts coast.

> *My own observations at Cape Cod, Gloucester, Cape Ann, Marblehead, Nantucket, &c., confirm the statement. And I can add, that in addition to the care of selection of places, great judgment is shown in the construction and*

The bank discovered by Henry Stellwagen is now part of an 842-square-mile national marine sanctuary. *Courtesy of NOAA.*

equipment of the boats and life-preservers, and that howitzers for throwing lines, and all the modern inventions for assisting shipwrecked crews to land, and numerous houses furnished with fuel, &c., for their preservation and comfort on reaching shore, have been provided by that admirable society, which also pays for the keeping of all the apparatus in good order, and causes a frequent inspection by Captain R.B. Forbes of all the details, with liberal power to repair and improve and re-arrange what may be necessary.

"Robert Bennet Forbes," wrote famed Boston maritime historian Samuel Eliot Morison, "had the most original brain, and the most attractive personality of any Boston merchant of his generation." He had already been decorated for bravery on his own, with a gold medal from the Humane Society, in 1849. He saw potential in Stellwagen's visitation and returned to see him again before he left the state. He was correct in his

instincts. Stellwagen had been sent not just to scout locations in the event that there might be lifeboats assigned to the coast. The lifeboats had already been designated for placement.

Henry Stellwagen wasn't looking for it, but he discovered the bank that now bears his name while finding places for lighthouses and lifesaving stations on the South Shore. *Courtesy of the U.S. Navy.*

Stellwagen wrote:

> *He agrees that all the most important sites are occupied and says it would require careful consideration to select others. I read to him the instructions to show him the views of the Treasury Department on the subject, and he evinced great interest and zeal in it. He made the very proposition that...the department should place the boats under the care of the society.*

Stellwagen quickly stated his opinion on the idea. "It would be decidedly the best course of action," he said, "should it be determined, to devote the four boats as originally proposed, to the service of the Massachusetts coast." Forbes had worked his magic on the lieutenant, but Bache was not convinced. The boats, though, did indeed end up in the hands of the Humane Society, a year and a half later.

Stellwagen finished other duties in the area, including surveying the Minot ledges off Scituate and Cohasset to determine the proper place to erect a new lighthouse, the old one having blown into the sea two years previous. The rocks, he mentioned in his report, were named "the Inner and Outer Minot, Hogshead Rock, East Willie and Shag Rock." He suggested the Inner Minot for the lighthouse, the advantages being "that it is greatly sheltered by the Outer Minot and much protected from the force of the sea; that a stone structure...can be erected, large enough at base, with a perfectly secure foundation on the rock." His assertion was that by using Inner Minot and adhering to strict construction guidelines, "the tower will be almost indestructible."

In 1854, Stellwagen returned to the Massachusetts coast for more routine U.S. Coast Survey work and cemented his legacy in the region forever. Bache wrote to Guthrie on November 24, 1854, of

> *the discovery, by Lieut. Comg. H.S. Stellwagen, in the entrance of Massachusetts Bay, of a bank, which must be of great importance to navigators as a guiding-mark. Stellwagen's Bank will rank in importance with Gedney's Channel, at the entrance of New York, and Davis' Shoal, on the highway to that mart from Europe and the eastern States, and will add another proof that important discoveries and developments are to be made by the Coast Survey, even in what may be called the beaten tracks of commerce and navigation.*

And so, while searching for sites for lifeboats and lighthouses on the South Shore, Lieutenant Henry S. Stellwagen discovered Stellwagen Bank.

1860: 1-4-3

Failure had to be admitted, but beyond that, there was work to do. The first Minot's Ledge Light had fallen into the sea on April 17, 1851, killing two men. Building the new lighthouse on the rocky ledge off the coasts of Cohasset and Scituate was never going to be about memorializing the lives of Joseph Wilson and Joseph Antoine; that would come later. Instead, it had to be about preventing the loss of more lives in the future. A lightship rode at anchor near the ledge warning mariners away from danger as the Army Corps of Engineers plotted its strategy.

Plans had to be drawn for something as yet untried in America. The first, ill-fated lighthouse boasted nine legs, eight in a circle with a central post, driven into the rock. The new light would have to be sturdier, more capable of dealing with the vicious allied powers of sea and storm. Colonel Joseph Totten, the chief engineer of the U.S. Army, designed the new lighthouse, handing off the plans to General Barton S. Alexander. Alexander tweaked the design slightly but essentially carried Totten's ideas forward.

Due to the disposition of the ledge itself, work had to be completed in frantic rushes. As the project began in 1855, Alexander and his men had to be mindful of two elements of the sea: tide and mood. The ledge became exposed enough for construction only at low tides. Moreover, even with a low tide, a rough sea would make work impossible. Calmness was a prerequisite to progress.

Progress came slowly. The engineers laid out courses of solid, Quincy granite (Cohasset's famed pink granite cracks unevenly) on the land-

The "New" Minot's Lighthouse, finished in 1860, stands strong today. *Courtesy of the author.*

tied Government Island, with plans of transferring them to the ledge for construction around an iron framework set for the purpose. That framework, though, collapsed in January 1857, to the dismay of Alexander. Not a witness to the incident, he believed that the wrought iron had fallen prey to the waves and felt that the plans for the stone lighthouse would have to be scrapped.

While most of the original "New" Minot's Lighthouse remains, the lantern room has been changed. *Courtesy of the U.S. Coast Guard.*

He was relieved to hear that instead of the sea, it was a ship colliding with the ledge that caused the damage. The accident restated, violently, the need for a proper lighthouse.

Six months later, the project recommenced from scratch. Oxen pulled the stones to locally hired barges that ferried them to the ledge in time for dead low tides. Workers unsuspecting of the power of sudden seas found themselves occasionally washed off the rock. Finally, in October 1858, a cornerstone was laid with appropriate speeches from state and national politicians. The idea of a new Minot's Ledge Lighthouse had finally turned the corner from concept to inevitable reality.

The workers set 1,079 stones. On June 29, 1860, the final stone was locked into place. On November 15, 1860, the light shone forth for the first time. The tower reached seventy-nine feet into the air from the ledge to the top of the lantern room. Below the lantern room were storerooms, living quarters and work areas. Below that, there was nothing but granite for forty feet, a solid mass anchoring the lighthouse to the ledge.

Since 1860, innumerable storms have tested Totten and Alexander's design. Spray from crashing waves often splashes higher than the lantern room, symbolizing, perhaps, Poseidon's wrath at man's defiance. In winter, such a storm leaves a white shadow of ice on the windward side of the lighthouse.

In the 1890s, the lighthouse received a new flash pattern: one flash, a pause, four flashes, a pause, three flashes. Poets and other romantics have translated the "1-4-3" as "I-Love-You," although the assignment of the pattern was purely random.

Lighthouses are on the road to obsolescence. The global positioning system now tells sailors where they are at all times. Where once they relied on celestial navigation for confirmation of location, now they rely on manmade bodies hurtling through the stars. Still, any sailor worth his salt will tell you that even with all of modern technology at his fingertips, it's still comforting to stick his head out of the wheelhouse, sight a lighthouse and know exactly where he is. Mariners have been doing it with Minot's for a century and a half, and they probably will for centuries more.

1860: The War Governor

It would never happen today. John Albion Andrew was pudgy and short and had a mess of curly hair sitting atop his bespectacled head. He graduated near the bottom of his Bowdoin class, yet he became one of the most influential Americans during the war that tore the country in half. Today, in an age when "image is everything," when politicians gain points for good looks, he wouldn't have stood a chance. But in the 1850s, a much more pragmatic time, when doers meant more than lookers, he was the right man for the job.

The people of Hingham knew that more than most, for he had lived among them. Born in Windham, Maine, and educated in that state, Andrew moved to Boston in 1837 to study law under Henry H. Fuller. He remained politically inactive, preferring to practice the art of debate in the courtroom, for the next two decades, despite a growing sentiment toward emancipation of slaves. While not a stumper or fist-banging campaigner, he did join the Whig Party, later helping to form the state's Free Soil Party. When that party failed, he helped form the Republican Party.

In 1848, he married Eliza Hersey, of the venerable Hingham family of that name. The South Shore community became his new home, the place where his heart resided, even in the turbulent years of the Civil War.

Finally, in 1857, Andrew stepped into the political realm, elected as a representative to the General Court. Two years later, he took the bold step of proclaiming John Brown, of the raid on Harper's Ferry, to be in the right, and on that wave he rode to the Republican nomination for governor of

The people of Hingham properly memorialized John Andrew in the Hingham Cemetery. *Courtesy of the author.*

Massachusetts. On the campaign trail, he stopped to address his friends in his beloved Hingham.

On September 3, 1860, John Albion Andrew led a procession of two to three thousand men, women and children from Loring's Hall to his own front lawn, and when the crowd settled, be began his address. "How dear to my heart are these fields, these hills, these spreading trees," he beamed in words and cadence paying respect to Samuel Woodworth's poem "The Old Oaken Bucket:"

> *This verdant grass, this sounding shore before you, where, now, for fourteen years, through summer heat, and sometimes, through winter storms, I have trod your streets, rambled through your woods, sauntered by your shores, sat by your firesides, and felt the warm pressure of your hands; sometimes*

teaching your children in the Sunday school, sometimes speaking to my fellow citizens…always with the cordial friendship of those who differed from me oftentimes in what they thought the radicalism of my opinions…speaking to willing ears—very much more willing to hear than my words were worthy to be listened to—on topics most interesting to your minds and convictions. Here, here I have found most truly a home of the soul, free from the cares and distractions, free from turmoil and doubts and anxieties and responsibilities of a careful and anxious profession. Here, too, dear friends, I have found the home of my heart.

During his speech, Andrew did not delve deeply into partisan politics, instead praising the people of Hingham for their willingness to speak out against injustice and to let their opinions be heard, hearkening back to the earliest settlers and their defiance of governmental oversight when they found it unfair. He ended his speech by saying, "All that I have, friends, to say to-night, bearing upon the political affairs of 1860, is that I hope all of you will be, as I know you are, 'bold men,' and that you will 'speak your minds.'" He then opened the doors of his house to the crowd, sharing food and drink with one and all.

Andrew knew that war was inevitable when most others were still unsure. As he campaigned, he kept that in mind. When he won the governorship by the widest margin ever to that point in history, one of his first priorities was the assembling of a standing army. In April 1861, when Confederate artillerymen fired on Fort Sumter and President Abraham Lincoln called for seventy-five thousand troops to defend Washington, Andrew sent Massachusetts men south within two days of the call, including troops from nearby Abington.

Characteristically, John Albion Andrew rolled up his sleeves and went to work, committing his life to the winning of the war and the emancipation of the slaves. The people of Hingham, especially, knew that as long as their townsman was in a position of prominence, those goals could be met.

1862: Fletcher Webster Pays the Price

Fletcher Webster had big shoes to fill, no matter how he looked at it. His father, Daniel Webster (yes, Marshfield's Daniel Webster) was a one-man army, a speaker and orator who publicly debated the hottest topics of the first half of the nineteenth century. As a young lawyer, Daniel fought for the rights of New England fishermen, which endeared him to the people of the region. A speech he gave on the fiftieth anniversary of the Battle of Bunker Hill helped propel him into the U.S. Senate. In all, he spent forty years in national politics. He was named secretary of state under three presidents and campaigned for the latter position himself, unsuccessfully.

Fletcher took up the challenge of being Daniel Webster's son with aplomb. Born in New Hampshire in 1818, he followed his father into the legal trade, graduating from Harvard in 1833 and soon thereafter passing the bar. While his father served as secretary of state, Fletcher served as his private secretary, gaining incredible experience. As chief clerk of the State Department, he hand-delivered the news of the death of former president William Henry Harrison to then-president William Tyler. He later moved to China, where he served as secretary of legation under Ambassador Caleb Cushing in 1843. In 1847, he served the Massachusetts legislature, and from 1850 to 1861, as the surveyor of the port of Boston. Just two years later, he would be carrying the Webster family banner alone, as his father passed onto the great debating grounds in the sky.

Fletcher's moment came in April 1861. A scant week after the bombing of Fort Sumter by Confederate troops in South Carolina, he called a meeting on State Street in front of the Merchants Exchange building. The crowd was

Marshfield's Fletcher Webster provided instant leadership for Massachusetts during the Civil War. *Library of Congress.*

so immense that the entire gathering moved to the rear of the Old State House, where Fletcher took to the balcony. "He was received with great favor," wrote William Schouler in *A History of Massachusetts in the Civil War.* "He said he could see no better use to which the day could be put than to show our gratitude to Divine Providence for bestowing upon us the best Government in the world and to pledge ourselves to stand by it and maintain it."

"Time presses," Fletcher stated. "The enemy is approaching the capital of the nation. It may be in their hands now. Promptness is needed. Let us show the world that the patriotism of '61 is not less than that of the heroes of '76; that the noble impulses of those patriot hearts have descended to us."

Within days, he raised a regiment of men ready to serve. His speech had encouraged sixteen companies of men, but the Twelfth Massachusetts Volunteer Infantry, the "Webster Regiment," could take only five. They drilled in Faneuil Hall until they overfilled the place, whence they moved to Fort Warren in Boston Harbor. On July 18, 1861, Governor John A. Andrew of Hingham reviewed the troops, the Honorable Edward Everett presented the unit its colors, on behalf of the ladies of Boston, and the following day, the Webster regiment left for war. They served picket duty in Frederick, Maryland, for nearly a year. Finally, in Virginia in April 1862, they encountered the enemy in the form of sporadic rifle fire.

General Gilman Marston of the Second New Hampshire Infantry met with Webster on August 30, 1862. Marston recalled:

I was lying under a fence rolled up in a blanket on the Bull Run battle field. It was the second day of the Bull Run battle. My own regiment, the Second New Hampshire Volunteers, had been in the fight the day before and had lost one third of the entire regiment in killed and wounded. While so lying by the fence someone shook me and said, "Get up here." In answer, I said without throwing the blanket from over my head, "Who in thunder are you?" The answer was made. "Get up here and see the Colonel of the Massachusetts Twelfth."

Webster and Marston talked of Fletcher's father, of trips he and his father took to New Hampshire for "fried apples and onions and pork," and soon, Webster's adjutant reported that his commanding officer wanted to see him.

"As he sat there on the blanket with me, he took hold of his left leg just below the knee with both hands and said, 'There. I will agree to have my leg taken off right there for my share of the casualties of this day.' I replied, 'I would as soon be killed as lose a leg, and the chances are a hundred to one that you won't be hit at all.'"

Webster and his men rushed to the right flank of the Union line, and as the afternoon wore on, the Confederates came in waves. The Twelfth Massachusetts fell back with the rest of the Union line, and in the confusion, Webster, shot through the wrist and breast, was captured and soon died.

1863: The South Shore at Gettysburg

In July 1863, Confederate general Robert E. Lee led his Army of Northern Virginia across the Pennsylvania state line in the boldest military move of the Civil War. The Southern forces for the first time invaded the North in force, clashing head-on with Union general George Meade's Army of the Potomac in a multi-day encounter that became known as the most important battle of the war. The place was Gettysburg, and the South Shore was there.

On July 1, 1863, Lee's army swept in on the Union men from the north and west, where the defenders fought bravely in just a foreshadowing of the epic story that was about to unfold. The Union soldiers fell back to high ground known as Cemetery Hill in the face of the advancing Confederates. Hingham felt the sting of loss that day, as Private Demerick Stodder took a musket ball to the forehead and died instantly at about sunset.

During the night, both sides received reinforcements. On July 2, Lee concentrated his strength at first on the left end of the defending line. There, defending the Emmittsburg Road with the First Massachusetts Volunteer Infantry Regiment alongside townsmen John Chessman, John Gardner, George Kilburn, Joseph Poole and Tom Tinsley, Hingham's Elijah Gill Jr. was struck with a musket ball in his side, a wound so debilitating that he was removed from the field. Captain Edward Humphrey of the Boston Volunteers, the Eleventh Massachusetts, also from Hingham, fared even worse, shot in four places, marked by Confederate troops as a target of importance. He survived the night only to die the following night in a

Peter Ourish's stone in the Hingham Cemetery tells the tale of his Civil War adventure by listing the battles in which he fought, including Gettysburg. *Courtesy of the author.*

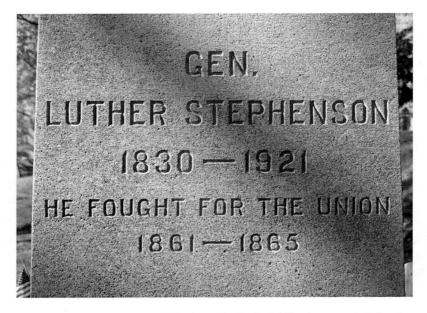

General Luther Stephenson of Hingham received a debilitating wound during the Battle of Gettysburg. *Courtesy of the author.*

field hospital. Private Daniel Horace Burr, also of the Eleventh, had been wounded once already at the Battle of Williamsburg on May 5, 1862. He returned to his unit in September of that year only to die facing the enemy at Gettysburg. His body was never recovered.

Elsewhere on the battlefield, other South Shore men fought bravely as the Confederates' concentration shifted from the left end of the line to the right. Isaac Damon, born in Scituate, fought with the Second Massachusetts. Colonel James L. Bates of Weymouth led the Webster Regiment, the Twelfth Massachusetts, named for its founder and lost hero, Marshfield's Fletcher Webster, son of Daniel, the great statesman. Nelson Lowell of Stoughton, a resident of Hanover after the war, saw the worst of the conflict. His unit, the Ninth Massachusetts Battery of Artillery, suffered terrible losses defending the Union line while reinforcements rushed forward. Lowell, a stable sergeant, begged his captain for the right to join the conflict, as he had been tucked into a position of safety to oversee the unit's horses. Captain John Bigelow placed him in charge of a detachment, "and when all his own men and horses had been shot, seemingly bearing a charmed life, he served as cannoneer with other detachments, while any were left, then, amid a shower of bullets, he helped 'right' one of Lieut. Milton's overturned [artillery] pieces and finally was held by his wounded horse among the enemy, until our lines advanced."

Lieutenant Colonel Luther Stephenson, who had taken command of the Thirty-second Massachusetts after the death of his commanding officer, took a rifle ball through the face that day. He returned to Hingham to recuperate but would be back on the battlefields by November.

On July 3, the Union pushed back, forcing Lee into one last move of desperation, a charge at the center of the Union line. The losses continued. William Hersey of Hingham received a wound that took him from the fight. Townsman John Elleson Snell took a bullet to the leg, and Sergeant Thomas Alonzo Carver took one to the arm. William Wallace Sprague of the Thirteenth Massachusetts, also of Hingham, hadn't been seen since the initial skirmishes on July 1. He had been taken prisoner and was on his way to Richmond, Virginia.

On July 4, the Confederates began their long march south. Their train of wounded stretched for fourteen miles.

As word of what had transpired reached the small towns of the South Shore, there were sharp pains of grief intermingled with wide-reaching waves of relief. Each town was contributing to the war. Plymouth would ultimately send 767 men; Duxbury, 236; Hanover, 169; Lakeville, 25; and etc. With dozens more South Shore men on the field at Gettysburg those days in early July, the death count could have been much worse.

Yet while the Union victory at Gettysburg may have "turned the tide," the war was not quite over.

1872: For Massachusetts's Citizen Soldiers

It would have been simple enough to dedicate a statue of Myles Standish to just Myles Standish in 1872. True, the wave of nostalgia for the Pilgrim forefathers would come later in the nineteenth century, when genealogical research boomed in an effort to prove American-ness in the face of what seemed like overwhelming immigration. But the people involved in the inspiration, creation, dedication and construction of the Myles Standish tower on Captain's Hill in Duxbury had broader notions in mind.

On August 17, 1871, the Reverend Josiah Moore led a gathered crowd at the Standish Memorial Exercises on the hill, land once owned by the military leader of the Plimoth settlement, in prayer, followed by the "Ode to Myles Standish," part of which goes as follows:

> *Fond hopes in Britain left,*
> *Of wealth and power bereft,*
> *Still, spirit free,*
> *You braved the ocean's roar,*
> *You wooed a frozen shore,*
> *That we might evermore*
> *Wed liberty.*

In May of the following year, the 252nd year after the landing of the Pilgrims, the Standish Monument Association formed. A month later, the state

More than anything else, Captain Myles Standish was a military man.

legislature gave the association its charter, making it an official body in the eyes of the State of Massachusetts. The association moved quickly. Boston architect Alden Frink drew up plans, and General Horace Binney Sargent, head of the First Massachusetts Cavalry during the Civil War, took the reins as president of the association. The advisory presidents included other famous Civil War men from New England, including General Joshua Lawrence Chamberlain of Maine and General Ambrose E. Burnside of Rhode Island. A board of fifty-four directors included General Benjamin F. Butler and numerous leading men from Duxbury and Kingston, even a few Bradfords and Standishes.

A relatively subdued groundbreaking took place atop the hill on August 9, 1872, following a luncheon at the ancient Standish homestead site at the end of Mayflower Avenue. The Duxbury selectmen were given the privilege of turning the first shovelfuls. "An opportunity for the ladies was given, when they joined in and handled the spade in good earnest," read the pamphlet distributed at the cornerstone laying two months later. "The Ancient and Honorable Artillery Company were represented; also the oldest Company of State Militia; also the families of Bradford, Brewster, Phillips, Pryor, Simmons, Allen, Ritchie, and many other visitors of the descendants of the Pilgrims."

The construction of the monument would be a tall task, from its height of 116 feet to the collection of stones requested—one from each New England state, one from each Massachusetts county, one from each military company in Massachusetts and a special one requested from the president of the United States, Ulysses S. Grant.

Invitations spread across the country for the October 7 cornerstone-laying ceremony. President Grant sent regrets, as did General William T. Sherman and poet Henry Wadsworth Longfellow. The cornerstone was prepared, with documents about the association, a history of Duxbury, the most recent editions of the *Hingham Journal, Old Colony Memorial* and other Massachusetts newspapers, a piece of "our Forefather's Rock" and "a piece of the hearth-stone of the original Myles Standish house taken from the ruins."

Approximately 350 members of the Ancient and Honorable Artillery Company left Boston's Faneuil Hall and marched to the Masonic Temple, where they took Grand Lodge dignitaries under escort and boarded eight Old Colony Railroad cars for Duxbury. They joined a crowd of between eight thousand and ten thousand who heard General Sargent give the dedication speech:

Myles Standish's monument stands for all of Massachusetts's citizen soldiers. *Courtesy of the author.*

> *Representatives from every organization of State soldiery, young heroes and martyrs of the coming time…assemble on this hill-side to establish a column that shall rise high above the headland and look far out forever over the Atlantic, in lasting commemoration of the trained citizen soldier, whose ashes lay somewhere near our feet, though his grave is lost to memory, and to whom this infant nation, which gratefully recognizes his services by granting to him this height of Captain's Hill, owed on many desperate occasions the only chance of life.*
>
> *We cannot forget that a citizen soldier guarded the cradle of the infant colony 250 years ago, and was her trusted servant for half a century of civil life. A citizen soldier led our fathers to victory against the British throne; and though assailed in his lifetime by ungrateful abuse, which he complained of as unjustifiable, even if applied to a notorious defaulter, is remembered as first in war, first in peace, and first in the hearts of his countrymen.*
>
> *Not only to the memory of Myles Standish, as the type of fearless and honest vigor in public service, as soldier and civilian, but also in a reverent*

spirit of remembrance and grateful honor to the citizen soldiers of New England, from the landing of the Pilgrims to the present hour, do we lay this cornerstone to-day.

It took twenty-six years to be finished, but in 1898, the Myles Standish Monument was completed in honor of Massachusetts's citizen soldiers.

1883: These Walls Can Talk

Historians and historic preservationists share a common dream. When they walk through the halls, corridors and rooms of ancient homes, fire stations, schools or town halls and think of all of the local historical characters that once followed the same paths, one recurring thought enters their mind: "Boy, if these walls could talk...."

Some walls do talk—in their own muted voices.

Scituate's Grand Army Hall began as a Baptist meetinghouse. Following the great religious awakenings of the early nineteenth century, that particular flock grew so populous in the small seaside town that it found it had the desire—and the funds—to purchase a lot of land at what is now called Scituate Center and to hire a local builder, Zeba Cushing, to build its members a place to practice their religion. Cushing did so in 1825, and for the next forty-one years, the Baptist Society met in their meetinghouse on Country Way.

America moved through great changes during those forty-one years. Locally, the Baptist Society outgrew the building and moved into a new church in North Scituate. The Civil War pulled many young Scituate men, mostly farmers, fishermen and Irish Mossers, to battlefields to the south, some of the men never returning to their beloved town. Most significantly, the concept of leisure time blossomed and soon ran rampant across the American landscape. In 1866, Joshua Jenkins purchased the old meetinghouse for $600 to convert it into a "hall," a word used at the time to describe a meeting place for parties and other forms of entertainment. Once dedicated

Scituate's Grand Army men marched in parades for every year that they could, but by the time World War I had come around, their numbers were thinning. *Courtesy of Scituate Historical Society.*

to the furtherance of religion and adherence to the straight and narrow path through life, the building became a place of revelry and temporary memory loss, where one could momentarily forget the responsibilities of family, work and religion.

Jenkins expanded the building and added a stage, renting his hall out to local groups. One of those groups, the local "post" of the Grand Army of the Republic, or GAR, began meeting in the hall in 1875. In 1883, it purchased the building and made it a permanent home.

The Grand Army formed in 1866, based loosely on Freemasonry, a fraternal organization joinable only with Union army credentials and Civil War experience. Nationally, the GAR became a potent political voice; between 1868 and 1908, no Republican presidential nominee could consider running for office without its backing. Locally, the GAR posts carried out a humbler mission.

Beginning in 1868, the men of the Grand Army donned their uniforms and marched throughout their hometowns every May 30 to decorate the

The Grand Army Hall in Scituate has been restored to its former glory. *Courtesy of the author.*

graves of their fallen brethren. This remembrance—concurrently started in the south for Confederate soldiers lost during the war—eventually grew into today's Memorial Day. As the old soldiers aged and passed on, fewer Grand Army men decorated more and more graves. They marched in every Memorial Day parade until they could march no more.

The members of the George W. Perry Post, No. 31, Grand Army of the Republic, actively engaged the Scituate community in their mission of eternal commemoration of the horrors of war and the sacrifices of local men. Patriotic speeches rang through the hall on nationalistic holidays as the post commander moved from man to man gathering the wartime stories and deeds of the men of the post in one common volume, a book now lovingly held by the Scituate Historical Society. As the years advanced, two new organizations joined in the work. The Women's Relief Corps organized meals and other events, and the Charles E. Bates Camp, Sons of Union Veterans, sought to raise funds for their fathers' care and the care of their Grand Army Hall.

Scituate's last surviving Civil War veteran, Francis Litchfield, died in 1936, and with him, so too did the George W. Perry Post. The Women's

Relief Corps and the Sons of Union Veterans continued their good work, but they too soon died out. In 1953, the Town of Scituate purchased the building and began renting it out to local groups.

A half-century later, in 1995, the 170-year-old building, once so full of life, was in line to be demolished. The Scituate Historical Society stepped in and asked that it be handed into their care. The following year, the society put a new roof on the hall to arrest ongoing water damage to the interior, and in 1997, the town made its pact with the society official, selling it for $1 with the provision that the society preserve it. Since that time, the society has raised more than $85,000 toward its restoration, including $20,000 from the sale of a local history book, *Images of America: Scituate*.

During the early stages of restoration, as local historians David Ball and David Corbin wandered through the ancient hall wishing the walls could speak, an employee of the contractor working on the building's interior made a startling discovery. Pulling away at the old interior walls to make room for construction anew, he was amazed to find a Civil War bayonet jammed into a post between the interior and exterior walls. The walls, in fact, could talk.

1884: A.W. Perry

He was born in Hanover but will forever be linked to Rockland. He started in shoes but moved into building management, electricity and steamships, becoming one of the largest property owners in Boston and the largest one in Rockland. And his name is still used throughout the South Shore today, representative of the business interests he created more than a century ago.

His name was Alonzo William Perry.

The year was 1884. Seeing the writing on the wall, Perry was leaving the shoemaking industry. He had graduated from the East Abington school system in 1867 (East Abington became Rockland in 1874), dabbled in higher education and entered the working world. After a year learning business practices at a wholesale house in Indianapolis, he returned to his father's shoe factory. Then, in 1872—two years after marrying his high school sweetheart, Isadora French—he purchased Samuel Reed Jr.'s shoe factory. He was twenty-two years old. But twelve prosperous years later, he knew it was time to move on. In 1884, local historian Charles Meserve noted that Perry's company earned $130,000 annually. But United Shoe was cornering the market, automating processes that gave them a benefit of speed and efficiency that the A.W. Perry shoemakers would never have. Perry had leased two floors of 125 Summer Street in Boston in order to sell his shoes in the city. When he left the shoe industry, he decided to sublease the space. He turned a quick profit.

With that single move, Perry laid a foundation that is as solid today as it was then. He quickly expanded, leasing other properties on Summer Street

Alonzo W. Perry started in shoes but eventually became one of Boston's great realtors. *Courtesy of Dyer Memorial Library.*

and then subleasing them to tenants of his own. The Church Green Building, 111 Summer Street, became an important cog in his growing property management machine. When Thomas Edison flipped the electricity switch in Boston in 1886, Perry was right there to join the electricity sales competition. He generated power in the basement of 111 Summer Street and sent it outward to purchasers. When the overhead wires choking the city streets of sunlight became too overwhelming, the city ordered them removed. Electricity became a sidelight business for Perry, as he could still sell power within its "block of origin," but without undertaking major steps to transfer it under the streets of the city, it would never again be a major factor in his business life.

Just as the light of the electricity game faded, though, the dream of steamship ownership became a reality. In 1904, Perry purchased the remains of Florida businessman Henry Plant's steamship line. At that time, it consisted of two ships: the *Halifax* and a former fruit steamer renamed *A.W. Perry*. Ill luck seemed to chase the ships wherever they went, especially the *Perry*, which ended up sunk at the head of Halifax Harbor in Nova Scotia. After about a decade, and after building his own luxury steamer, the *Evangeline*, Perry and, by that time, his sons Winthrop, Herbert and Butler, stepped ashore for good, back to their real estate concerns.

By the 1920s, A.W. Perry was not only one of Boston's largest property owners, but Rockland's as well. As early as 1907, he owned sixty properties in town, including most of the prominent business blocks on Union Street, paying $3,000 of the $80,000 in taxes collected annually. His success had given him freedom to roam, to see the world. Newspaper reporters found him in exotic locales, from Hawaii to Egypt to Scotland, and sought quotes on the economic doings of the day. But no matter where he went, his heart always remained tied to his hometown.

In 1914, A.W. Perry furnished the pulpit for the Rockland Baptist Church. In 1916, he added the French Home for Aged Women at 148 South Union Street, the former home of his wife's deceased parents and the building in which he and Isadora had been married in 1870. In 1921, upon the passing of his beloved wife, he donated an Estes organ to the church and the following year added a church bell.

Perhaps becoming aware of his own mortality, Perry incorporated his business in 1922, naming his son Hebert as the company's president. When Perry died in 1928, he left behind an empire—one that would be severely tested by the Great Depression but would evolve fluidly with the times. In 1960, when the city of Boston began licensing, Herbert Perry, known as the dean of the city's real estate world, was granted real estate license number one. A.W.'s sons ran the company until death claimed them; their children followed them, and so on. A.W. Perry Inc. is, above all else, a family company.

Circumstances have brought the story full circle. Today, A.W. Perry Inc. owns numerous properties in Boston but has returned to the South Shore. Residents of Kingston's Conifer Green, businessmen and women who report to work each day at South Shore Park in Hingham, diners at Scarlet Oak Tavern at Hingham's Queen Ann's Corner and even passersby who glance in the windows of the Phoenix Block in Rockland can link their stories back to that town's self-made man and champion philanthropist, A.W. Perry.

1887: Henry Turner Bailey

He hated tobacco and alcohol and their effects on human life. He distrusted dogs. And he only warmed to cats in midwinter, when they were unable to get at the songbirds with which he so loved to commune. His daughter Margaret even remembers hearing him once shout in frustration the harshest words he ever put together: "Baked rabbits on the half-shell!" When it came down to it, Henry Turner Bailey had one of the gentlest souls Scituate has ever known.

He was a townie, born in North Scituate, raised in North Scituate, and when the time came, he bought a patch of blueberry thickets on which to build his own house in North Scituate, Trustworth. He graduated as valedictorian of his 1882 Scituate High School class. One tale, perhaps apocryphal but certainly plausible, holds that his teachers had to pin his sleeves to his seat to keep him from drawing when there was arithmetic to be studied (a topic he hated). His daughter claimed that he would feign interest in his geography book, using it as a cover for his sketching. Seven years later, he married his fourth-grade sweetheart, Josephine, who graduated second to him in academic achievement in 1882. While still unmarried, she taught school in the Egypt section of town (married women were deemed too impure to teach children in those days) while he pursued his passion for art education.

Upon graduation from the Massachusetts Normal Art School, Bailey landed a role as the head of drawing in the Lowell public schools. His star was just beginning to rise. From 1887 to 1903, he worked as the state's—and the nation's—only supervisor of drawing. During that time, his zestful

Right: Scituate's Henry Turner Bailey represented the United States at international art events on a regular basis. *Courtesy of Carol Miles.*

Below: While most people would record their thoughts about their childhoods in words, Henry Turner Bailey decided to sketch his. *Courtesy of Carol Miles.*

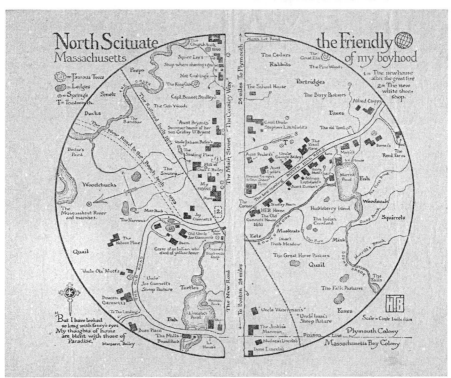

enthusiasm led him into the lecture circuit, mostly to talk about art and its many themes. He started with a few talks on Martha's Vineyard and soon expanded to the rest of Massachusetts, his beloved Scituate always being a preferred venue.

When in town, he contributed tremendously to the cultural life of the community. He drew the town seal in 1900. He created the patterns for the stained-glass windows for the First Baptist Church. He even designed the Seaside Chapel at North Scituate Beach (in 1888, he had even drawn up the plans for Trustworth, giving them to his Uncle Waldo to bring to life). Whenever he was around during the town meeting, he was voted town moderator, a position typically filled on the day of the meeting in those days. He served as surveyor of lumber, and he co-founded the Peirce Memorial Library, the Hatherly Country Club and the Scituate Historical Society.

Beginning in 1898, though, his life would be spent, in significant amounts of time, outside of town. That year, for the first time, Bailey accepted an invitation to act as the U.S. delegate to the International Art Congress, held in France. He played that role five more times. He lectured in every state in the union and in seventeen European countries, often bringing "Jo" and the kids with him.

From 1903 to 1917, he followed a dream that had long eluded him. Sensitive to the needs of art teachers around the country, he founded the *School Arts Book*, later to be called the *School Arts Magazine*. He wrote eight books on art, inspired by the trees of Scituate and its sunrises, wildflowers and wild birds. When home, he wandered through the woods and fields endlessly, eventually founding the South Shore Nature Club so that he could share his love of the wilds of Scituate with others.

He spent fifteen years as the director of the Cleveland School of Art, his summers punctuated for many years with teaching at Chautauqua in New York.

Sadly, his energy ran out when, on a trip to Chicago in 1931, he fell and broke a kneecap while running to cross a street. After several weeks in the hospital, a blood clot took him in his sleep, robbing Scituate of one of its most beloved sons on Thanksgiving Day. Eulogies poured forth, perhaps none more poignant than that written by Rebecca Richmond in *Chautauqua: An American Place* fourteen years after his death: "He brought a philosopher's approach to his work; art, he said, would lead to a lifelong interest in almost anything."

A local writer signing off as G.C.T. (possibly George C. Turner) lamented Scituate's true loss: "With a tremendous energy, Mr. Bailey vitalized every path which his footsteps trod. His love for his native town was overpowering, and he impressed this feeling upon everyone whom he met. He was one of the truest exponents of local patriotism that the South Shore has ever produced."

1892: A Bridge at Powder Point

The Civil War had just ended, and the pace of life was about to quicken on the South Shore of Boston. The Industrial Revolution was changing the world, separating economic classes and delivering Americans to formerly inaccessible places and into realms of self-discovery they never thought possible.

In 1869, three men—David Cushman, George W. Wright and Allen Prior—petitioned the Massachusetts state legislature for the right to form a corporation with the ultimate goal of building a "pile bridge across the waters of the harbor of Duxbury, commencing at some point on Powder Point, so called, and extending in a straight line to Salt House Beach, so called." The state granted them their wish, allowing them use of the name Duxbury Bridge Company. Furthermore, the new corporation was given the right to extract tolls: "for each horse and rider, ten cents; for each chaise, cab, carryall, buggy or sleigh drawn by one horse, fifteen cents; for each carriage, coach, phaeton or sleigh drawn by two horses, twenty cents; for each additional horse, five cents; for each cart, wagon, sled, sleigh, or other carriage of burden, drawn by one beast, fifteen cents; and for each additional beast, five cents; for each horse without a rider, and for neat cattle, asses and mules, five cents each; for each single person, two cents."

That bridge was never built.

Eighteen years later, in 1887, a new corporation, the Gurnet Bridge Company, received the state's blessing to take on the project never completed by the Duxbury Bridge Company: to build a span from Powder Point to

Although the Powder Point Bridge has been reconstructed several times, some parts have been recycled. The osprey-nesting platform at Hicks Point in Duxbury is made from an original Powder Point Bridge plank. *Courtesy of the author.*

"Salter's Beach, so-called." George Wright, who had purchased Duxbury Beach in that year, had never given up on his dream. His nephew, William Wright, had dreams of his own, of developing that land by building 263 houses on the sandy stretch. But there were already plenty of reasons to take the long trip down the beach road to the Gurnet. Between 1840 and 1860, the Old Sebastopol, a dance hall, provided mirth in the night at the Gurnet. George Hall opened his pavilion around 1880, and the Boardman family, after a land swap with Hall, reopened it as the Gurnet House in 1884. A federal lifesaving station had opened at the point in 1874, to join the twin Gurnet Lighthouses, built in 1768, in defending local mariners against the ravages of the sea. They shared the point with the earthwork remains of the Revolutionary War–era Fort Andrew. By October 1892, the 2,200-foot bridge to the beach had been built of oak piles and a "hard pine" floor, complete with a draw in the middle for the passage of boats up and down the channel. The bridge shortened the terrestrial trip from the villages of Duxbury to the beach (previously by way of Canal Street in Marshfield) by seven hours.

That bridge is not the one that stands today.

The "Long Bridge" or "Half-Mile Bridge" held up well through time. The financial panic of 1893 led to the quashing of William Wright's dreams of summer cottages along the shore, and by 1904, Plymouth County had taken control of the bridge. Although the 1913 report of the state highway commission noted that "automobiles are excluded from the so-called Gurnet Bridge," by the 1920s, said Frederick T. Pratt, "every pleasant Sunday all of the bridge and adjacent Powder Point streets were completely lined with parked automobiles."

Major repairs were made in 1917, 1928, 1936, 1937 and 1938. On July 6, 1939, at a special town meeting, the people of Duxbury voted, 71 to 17, to take control of the bridge from the county. The town did so in 1941. By 1971, short-term repair estimates reached $240,000, while long-term recommendations by an independent consultant included replacing the bridge entirely. By 1982, inspectors estimated that the bridge had two years left. It had three.

At 5:00 a.m. on June 11, 1985, fire broke out on the bridge, destroying about seventy-three feet of the planks and pilings. Repairs made over the course of five weeks proved inadequate, and just three days after reopening in July, the bridge was closed indefinitely.

For the next twenty months, design and construction of a new Powder Point Bridge was undertaken by Universal Engineering of Boston and

Harbor Marine Corporation of Rhode Island. It would be a $2.98 million project. In a pioneering move, the engineering firm called for the use of exotic woods, marine borer–resistant basralocus from Suriname (which made it out of the country just before the ports closed in the face of a civil war) and fire-resistant bongossi from West Africa. The bridge that stands today is wider than the old bridge by nearly four feet, has a fifteen-ton capacity (as compared to the old bridge's four-ton capacity) and is slightly arched to allow for water runoff and easy passage underneath for boats. On its opening day, August 29, 1987, five hundred people walked across the bridge.

The old bridge has not completely disappeared. For those folks nostalgic for it, a walk at the Daniel Webster or North River Wildlife Sanctuaries in Marshfield may be in order, where rough-cut benches made from the original pilings wait silently for passersby. Out at Hicks Point along Bay Road in Duxbury, the ospreys that have nested there successfully for so many years do so on a platform mounted atop a pole that once served as a plank on the bridge. After all, this is New England, where thriftiness is an art form.

1893: Mr. Bradley's Horses

Leaving North Weymouth, or, as it was historically known, "Old Spain," wrote Robert Derrah in his *Official Street Railway Guide for Eastern Massachusetts and Rhode Island* in 1899, "the cars cross Weymouth Back River, so-called to distinguish it from 'Fore' River…and then run though a pretty wooded district belonging to the Peter Bradley estate. Off to the left, a line runs to Fort Point and to the Bradley Fertilizer Works." Author Elizabeth Coatsworth added in her *South Shore Town* that "the wide fields and woods of the Bradley place were a green bar across the spread of the industrial world forever pushing out from Boston. When one crossed the bridge over Back River, one came upon country again, and beyond Mr. Bradley's, Hingham began as a separate and integrated town."

In these lush meadows and on these bucolic fields, Peter Bradley made American history.

The arrival of the Bradley family to Hingham was not, at first, welcomed by the townsfolk en masse. Peter's father, William L. Bradley, was one of the country's greatest manufacturers of chemical fertilizers and during the Civil War had set up what grew to be the largest plant of its type in the world, on Weymouth Neck. The owner was gentlemanly enough, but his plant was, in the words of Lorena and Francis Hart in *Not All is Changed: A Life History of Hingham*, "a mixed blessing, especially in warm weather when windows were open." The works expanded onto the Hingham side of the Back River, but a technical solution to the problem was found, sparing Hingham's residents and visitors from the olfactory assault.

With money to spare, thanks to his father's entrepreneurially gained wealth, young Peter Bradley began to indulge his passion for horses, building a massive farm with stables, polo grounds and a racetrack on his Hingham lands. It wasn't until 1893, though, that he found his true passion. The Chicago World's Fair held that year opened his eyes to purebred Arabian horses, desert born and trained, mythically created by Allah out of the winds of the four corners of the compass. Strong, handsome, fast and intelligent, they were under tight control by Arab governments, which forbade their export from the Middle East. But due to a bizarre series of events that led to the auctioning of several mares and studs of the Hamidie Hippodrome Society in a mortgage settlement after the exposition, Bradley acquired enough of them to become one of the first breeders of purebred Arabian horses in the United States.

His passion was shared by another young man attending the fair, political cartoonist Homer Davenport. Davenport visited the Hingham Stock Farm, as it came to be known, in 1898, and by 1906, the two men were in business together under the name Davenport Desert Arabian Stud. That year marked an important step forward in the American breeding of Arabian horses. Bankrolled by the retiring Bradley, who tended to speak little and remain entrenched in the background, and diplomatically supported by President Theodore Roosevelt (who Davenport had supported though his cartoons, including a famous image of Uncle Sam saying, "He's good enough for me!" in time for the 1904 presidential election), Davenport visited the Middle East in search of breeding stock. He returned with twenty-seven more mares and studs to bolster the stock of the newly organized joint firm.

Davenport, though, had little opportunity to enjoy the venture. For the next six years, horses moved between the Hingham Stock Farm and Davenport's farm in Morris Plaines, New Jersey, ensuring efficient use of the breeding stock available. In 1908, he and Bradley helped form the Arabian Horse Club of America, but in 1912, tragedy struck. Waiting on the New York waterfront for the survivors of the *Titanic* disasters to arrive, Davenport contracted pneumonia and died. Most of the stock at his New Jersey farm was transferred to Hingham.

Peter Bradley continued the work of his farm, his last foal, Carolstone, arriving in 1925. Concurrently, he supported his community in several ways. He donated a triangle of land at the intersection of Route 3A and Lincoln Street on which the town built a police station. When the state experimentally designated five thousand acres of nearby land as the Hingham Reservation for wildlife in 1915, the Division of Fish and Game supplied food to feed the wild fowl, "and Peter Bradley, Esq., furnished in addition many hundred pounds of grain, and instructed his employees to expend as much care on the wild birds as on his live stock."

Between 1917 and 1925, Bradley sold much of his breeding stock to Japanese interests and breeders in California and New Hampshire. In 1926, a Hingham Stock Farm bred stud, Jadaan, then under the ownership of W.K. Kellogg of Battle Creek, Michigan, the breakfast cereal king, appeared on the silver screen with Rudolph Valentino in *Son of the Sheik*, one of six films in which the Arabian appeared. Peter Bradley died in 1933.

There is no marker for Bradley's farm, no place to which fans of Arabian horses can today travel to pay homage to one of the men responsible for the horse's American saga. But Hingham residents who know their history see the large stone pillars at the entrances to Bradley Hill Road and Bradley Park Drive, the development at Bradley Woods and even the new development at what to most is now the "old shipyard" site and know that these lands once belonged to an American horse-breeding pioneer.

1897: Hull vs. Hingham

The towns of Hingham and Hull have been at it since the seventeenth century. By the 1640s, they were feuding over ownership of the southernmost sands of Nantasket Beach, a row so dire that it required settlement by the General Court in Boston. Hingham descended to calling the Hull settlement a "moon village at the end of the earth." There are no written records of what the salty fishermen of Hull called Hingham, but one only needs let the imagination wander.

The Hull versus Hingham feud has manifested itself in myriad ways over the centuries—politically, through the editorial columns of rival newspapers and even by means of matching their young men's sporting prowess. Perhaps no better demonstration of the depth of the contentious nature of the communities' relationship can be found in the pages of history than the events of Thanksgiving Day 1897.

On that day, two dozen of the beloved sons of the neighboring towns strode out onto the slippery tundra of the Hingham Agricultural Grounds wearing baggy pants, horsehair shirts and with wildly growing hair, vowing to settle the score between the communities on the football gridiron. The pants (no tackling below the waist), the shirts (slick enough to allow a ball carrier to elude the grasp of a tackler) and the hair (grown out since July as extra padding) comprised the standard uniform of the day for an American football player.

In fact, Thanksgiving Day 1897 marked the third clash of the rival teams in recent times. A game earlier in the year had ended in a scoreless tie,

Playing football in the 1890s meant wearing horsehair shirts, growing one's hair long from midsummer on and donning a nose guard if necessary. *Courtesy of Fort Revere Park & Preservation Society.*

while Hull had won the 1896 Thanksgiving Day game 10–0. Hingham claimed Hull had stocked its roster with college stars. The 1897 Hull team outweighed their Hingham rivals by a large margin. Such always seemed to be the case. When Hull put out the challenge the following year to play any team averaging no more than 125 pounds a player, it found only one opponent all autumn, Thayer Academy, which they beat 11–0. Duxbury, which had originally agreed to send a team, backed out when it realized it would be seriously outsized by Hull.

At 10:00 a.m., referee George James called for the game to start. The previous year's referee, Dr. William Harvey Litchfield, a once and future state representative from Hull, had not been invited back on the basis of football incompetence. The *Hingham Journal* reported on December 4, 1896, that Litchfield had actually allowed Hull to complete a forward pass, an incorrigible play that would remain illegal for the next decade on all football fields in the United States.

Hull kicked off to the ten-yard line, but Hingham could not move the ball past the thirty-five. Hull lost possession quickly, turning the ball over on downs, and Hingham began to march steadily downfield. Under the

FROM PLYMOUTH ROCK TO QUINCY GRANITE

current rules system at the time, without forward passes, every play looked like third down and one yard to go. The only options were to run the ball up the middle or around the ends. However, since there were no rules about the number of men in motion, teams could form "flying wedges," with ten blockers surrounding the ball carrier, and bash their way downfield with a running start. The most popular way to stop the flying wedge was to dive under the lead blocker and open a hole in front of the runner for other defenders to run through. The most daring way was to leap over the lead blocker and come crashing down on the ball carrier.

Hingham's mass-momentum plays could not be stopped, though. The *Hull Beacon* reported that "Hingham secured the ball and worked it down the field by superb interference," of course noting that Hingham had "the advantage of going down hill." The last fact was conspicuously absent from the *Hingham Journal's* coverage. The *Journal's* more detailed account described the inevitable scoring play by saying that Hingham "pushed Keenan through the line for a touchdown."

Hingham could not convert its goal after touchdown, and at halftime, after twenty-five minutes of play, the score stood at 4–0 in favor of Hingham.

To start the second half, Hingham kicked off, but the ball glanced off the kicker's foot and skidded up the middle of the field, where Hull downed the ball on the fifty-five-yard line. Hull could do nothing to advance the ball, though, and Hingham took over on downs.

Hingham immediately called a guards-back play, with fantastic results. Before the snap of the ball, the quarterback called for his two guards to line up behind him in the backfield. The tackles and ends then tightened up their formation, and the ball was snapped and handed to one of the guards, who barreled down the field. "It was a most satisfying sight to the Hingham rooters to see him gain ten yards with as many Hull men on his back as there was room for any back to possibly hold," reported the *Journal*.

With about ten minutes to play, "Dick" Hayes of Hull was knocked unconscious. The young Harvard law student was forced to leave the game, replaced by Stillman Dexter Mitchell. "Bugs" Mitchell, as he was known, had lost most of his front teeth in a similar situation in the 1896 game but had stayed in until the final whistle.

Hingham retained possession of the ball for the remainder of the half, as Hull valiantly defended its goal. When the final whistle sounded, the ball sat six inches from the goal line. A moral victory for Hull perhaps, but the game was lost.

Ten minutes later, when Hayes woke up, the Hull team left for home. Apparently, it had not planned to leave in defeat. "Somebody of prying nature," wrote the *Journal*, "discovered concealed beneath the seats of the coach quite a number of those useful household articles, brooms. Of course, the Hull boys, knowing in what condition the ground would be, brought them along for the obvious purpose of cleaning the field. Nobody could be evil-minded enough to even imagine that they, on the strength of their confidence to win the game, had brought them to 'do the town.'" Apparently, taunting after a sweep was not yet illegal either.

As the Hull eleven trudged back up the peninsula, they vowed to get their revenge on the next Thanksgiving Day. Most importantly, rather than settling any score, the 1897 Hull versus Hingham contest had simply added fuel to the ever-burning fire that raged between the towns.

1900: Copper King

Before Thomas W. Lawson came along, Scituate was a town of farmers, Irish Mossers, salt-hayers and, at least historically, shipbuilders and ship captains. The town had remained off the beaten track for more than two centuries, even passing a law forbidding the keeping of out-of-town guests overnight in 1667. This rule may have been forged as a protective measure against the spread of smallpox, but the identity of Scituate as a tight-knit and private community remains today.

In the spring of 1900, the town was struggling to get back on its feet. The ravages of the Portland Gale of November 26–28, 1898, had changed the community forever. Gone was the barrier beach between Third and Fourth Cliffs, blasted outward during the height of the storm, meaning the North River had a new outlet to the sea. Gone were one thousand barrels of *chondrus crispus*, the red algae known as Irish Moss that was the most important exportable product the community produced. Although many of its famous old landmarks remained—including the Old Oaken Bucket House, named for Samuel Woodworth's poem, and Old Scituate Lighthouse, the scene of the famous "American Army of Two" incident during the War of 1812, when Rebecca and Abigail Bates reportedly chased off the British Navy with a fife and a drum—much of the town would never be seen again.

From the ashes of the damaged community would arise an estate unrivaled in the history of the South Shore region. According to local legend, Copper magnate Thomas W. Lawson chose the site of his future Egypt home while on a carriage ride from his summer estate in Cohasset with his wife, Jeannie Augusta

Thomas W. Lawson's Dreamwold turned Scituate upside-down. *Courtesy of Scituate Historical Society.*

(Goodwillie) Lawson. She pointed to the undulating hills and the views of the sea, and through the briars and across the rocky landscape, she envisioned a future cozy, secluded family home. But Lawson, as usual, thought bigger.

At eight, Lawson lost his father to complications from wounds suffered during the Civil War. Wanting to help his mother, he took a job in a bank, and before he became a teenager, he began speculating in the stock market. At seventeen, he gained and lost a small fortune and at thirty became a millionaire. In the 1890s, he first fought against Standard Oil and then joined them as one of their hotshot agents. In 1897, he took control of Amalgamated Copper, owned by Standard Oil, and led the charge to enormous stock profits. By age forty-three, when he arrived in Scituate, Lawson was worth an estimated $50–60 million, having become the "Copper King" of the United States.

In November 1900, word began to spread that Lawson intended to do something big in Scituate. Newspaper publisher and gossip hound Floretta Vining wrote in the *Scituate Light* (which doubled as the *Hull Beacon*, *Cohasset*

Tom Lawson believed in horses, cattle and English bulldogs. *Courtesy of Scituate Historical Society.*

Sentinel and six other newspapers with different mastheads), "I hear Tom Lawson has bought fifty acres and intends to improve it very much. What a future this town has in store for it."

Workmen removed rocks by the wagonload before laying out roads, constructing buildings, installing a system of electric lights, erecting six miles of Kentucky horse farm–style fencing and planting acres of trees and shrubs. "It is the beginning of another of Thomas W. Lawson's great enterprises," announced the *Scituate Light* in June 1901, "and the once desolate and unattractive brushwood patch will soon be the home of blooded horses and one of the great points of interest on the shore."

When completed, the buildings on the estate, all of Dutch colonial-style architecture with gambrel roofs, were unlike anything Scituate had ever seen. The main racing stable stretched 800 feet in length, while the riding academy, finished in just fifty-six days, boasted an oval 108 feet by 170 feet. The blacksmith had room in his shop to shoe eight horses at a time.

Lawson filled Dreamwold Farm, a come-to-life version of his childhood fantasy, with 300 of the finest head of cattle, 200 of the country's most lauded horses and 150 of the best show dogs his buyers could find. He had a predilection for English bulldogs, calling the breed the "gent of dogdom." To watch over them all, he hired one hundred men, led by the estate manager, George Pollard.

The main house, which faced the sea with a view of Minot's Light to the north and Duxbury to the south, featured a billiards room, high-backed cane chairs with leather cushions in the great hall, a Tiffany pumpkin-globe lamp dangling above the dining room table and carved gnomes representing various genres of writing on the bookcases in the library.

Lawson's superstitious side showed throughout the grounds. Believing that elephants with upturned snouts symbolized good luck, he had three thousand such representations on the estate, paying one man to count them each night. Believing in the power of the number three, he ordered Lawson Tower, the Rhine River–style covering for the Scituate Water Company's new standpipe across from his back door, to be constructed in numbers divisible by the number: 123 steps to the top, its apex reaching 153 feet, with three decorative finials, etc.

Though one could never say that the estate was ever finished, Thomas W. Lawson's Dreamwold Farm brought a fantasy world to sleepy Scituate and the South Shore—one that they may never experience again.

1904: Wildflowers of Plymouth and Vicinity

It must have been wonderful to live in the world of Catherine Elliott Hedge. She lived in a Plymouth that was preparing for the grandest celebration of its settled history, in a time when the notion of being a *Mayflower* descendant was never more important. In the latter half of the nineteenth century and first decades of the twentieth, a time in which Americans were overwhelmed with immigration and societal diversification, tracing lineage to the Pilgrims marked unbreakable American-ness. All of those roads led through Plymouth.

Yet, as most of America waded through a genealogical sea, knee-deep in great-aunts and uncles and swimming far from the shoals of shady grandfathers and unladylike great-grandmothers, Catherine Elliott Hedge set herself on a study of a different kind. Her life's passion was not for human achievements, but those of Mother Nature.

The Industrial Revolution paved the way for Americans to follow their favored pursuits in the late 1800s. The old adage "idle hands do the Devil's work" was taking a beating, as notions of leisure time and—heaven forbid—vacations gripped the American public or, at least, that portion of it with disposable income. Money was not an issue for Catherine. On October 11, 1871, she married William Hedge, also of Plymouth. They were born just three days apart in February 1840, she the last of six children. He trained at Boston Latin School and thereafter Harvard University. Upon graduation in 1862, he, like most young men of his age, enlisted to fight in the Civil War. He served for five months with the Forty-fourth Massachusetts Volunteer

Right: Catherine Elliot Hedge loved wildflowers, including the pink lady's slipper. *Courtesy of the author*.

Below: Starflowers burst early on spring, then retreat once the trees leaf out and the canopy blocks the sunlight from hitting the forest floor. *Courtesy of the author*.

Infantry Regiment, commissioned as a first lieutenant and completing his duty in North Carolina. He passed the bar three years later, embarking on a career in the legal field. In him she found a kindred spirit. His fiftieth anniversary Boston Latin School class report noted that, aside from his active work on behalf of the Plymouth Public Library, "for over twenty years he has been interested in the Old Colony Natural History Society of Plymouth." In 1872, Catherine gave birth to daughter Lucia. In 1876, she and William welcomed twin boys, William and Henry, to the world.

Life was good. In 1888, Catherine and William were each listed in the book *Twenty Thousand Rich New Englanders*, a compilation of the region's residents who paid more than $100 in taxes annually.

Although Plymouth was a bustling hub in the latter half of the nineteenth century, home to one of the busiest cordage companies in the world, multiple other factories of numerous varieties and an active waterfront, it was still a place of wide-open spaces, rolling farmland and deep woods. And that is where Catherine Elliott Hedge went to work on the simple list that would become her legacy, her greatest gift to the people of Plymouth: *Wild Flowers of Plymouth and Vicinity, 1804–1904.*

She wandered the woods and surveyed the swamps, bounded down dusty dirt roads, meandered into meadows and scoured the sands of Plymouth Beach. "She spent many hours searching out plants in their various habitats, sometimes employing the assistance of local children," says historian James Baker. Another longtime Plymouth historian related her memories of Catherine's outings. Baker continues:

> *Rose Briggs remembered being a member of these summer expeditions as a girl, being driven in a wagon with Mrs. Hedge along woodlot roads in quest of elusive blossoms. They would stop from time to time, and the children would be told to get down and go into whatever swamp or thicket was at hand to look for a particular plant. They would then make their way as best they could, stepping over cat briars and pushing through the scrub brush and trying to avoid muddy places until they found the desired flower, just as it had been described. They then struggled back, scratched and sweating and swatting away slow-buzzing flies to deliver the prize. Mrs. Hedge, sitting comfortably beneath her parasol, would graciously receive the specimen and tell her driver to proceed to the next venue.*

Catherine's list included the dominant tree species of the region: the oaks, maples and the ubiquitous *Pinus rigida*, or pitch pine. She noted the rarer species: the shagbark hickories, American hornbeams and swamp willows. She gladly added staghorn "sumach" and poison ivy alongside silvery cinquefoil, white-topped aster and red cardinal flower. She noted invasive or transplanted species like black henbane, snow-on-the-mountain and English oak as "escaped." She bent low for the beauty of the lady's slipper and the hidden treasure of the *Arisaema triphyllum*, which she knew as the Indian turnip but what we know as the Jack-in-the-pulpit. She eagerly awaited the first fuzzed-out pussy willow of spring, and delighted in the last flower of the New England year to bloom, on the wetland denizen witch hazel.

She published her work in 1904, providing local floraphiles with a checklist of delights to find on a summer's day. Catherine Elliott Hedge passed away on June 15, 1916, preceding her husband by almost three years, but left South Shore residents of today a snapshot of the natural life of Plymouth as the old town approached its tercentennial celebration.

1906: A Ballgame on Peddocks

T he notion came out of the Hull Old Home Week celebration of 1904: why not get some of the old Boston baseball players together and have them play an exhibition game on Peddocks Island? The thought made John Irwin, the proprietor of the Island Inn, furrow his brow and think. Would the boys turn out?

Irwin, of course, had connections. Born in Toronto in 1861, the old third baseman had made his professional debut on May 31, 1882, for the Worcester Ruby Legs. He then scrapped through the next nine years for the Boston Reds, Philadelphia Athletics, Washington Nationals, Buffalo Bisons and Louisville Colonels. His brother Arthur, a middle infielder, had put together a fifteen-year career. Yes, thought John, this could work.

It took a few years to come to fruition, but in August 1906, the boys started to wash ashore. "They weren't invited," said the *Boston Globe*, "but some one has said, 'Come on, boys, let's get together.' And so they came, and they're jolly glad they did."

There was no plan other than the game itself, to be played between the "Old-Timers" and the "Colts," and dinner at the inn, as informality ruled. But Irwin promised a good time. To start things off, Julian B. Hart, a mover and shaker in the building of the Players League, raised the pennant won by the Boston nine in 1890 to the top of the Inn's flagpole, throwing memories of baseball glories past to the breeze for the old players and the rooters who'd turned out to thank them for their inspirations.

They took to the field. Dupee Shaw took the mound for the Old-Timers, eighteen years past retirement, toeing the rubber against a nine composed of younger retirees, matched up against Jere McNamara. On this day, the young bucks were no match for the prowess of Braintree's Jack Manning, playing in his straw hat, tie and suspenders, an eleven-year veteran who, after stealing only six bases in the first ten years of his career, swiped twenty-four for the 1886 Baltimore Orioles; future Hall of Famer Tommy McCarthy of Boston, who stole two bases on this day, hearkening back to his 1888 campaign with the St. Louis Browns, when he pilfered ninety-three; and "Dandy" George Wood, who appeared in the top ten in home runs six times in the National League in the 1880s and was a member of the 1890 Players League champions.

With the game concluded, a 9–3 drubbing by the elders, the players retreated to the Inn, though various other pick-up games were in action around the island. Mike Reagan's German Band led the singing of "The Wearing of the Green," "the only tune the band could play without its notes, which the musicians could not see very well because of the strong light and Reagan's hospitality." John Irwin's staff, aided by the fans who had traveled from the city to leap at the chance to rub elbows with the famous stars of their day, put on a fish dinner the likes of which the people of the South Shore knew well but, as the *Globe* said, was "such as one reads about but seldom gets next to."

Mike Reagan, not just bandmaster but also umpire for the day's game and master of ceremonies, called for after-dinner speeches. The "Sunflowers," as the gang came to call itself, spoke glowingly of the national pastime, its past, present and future. Charlie Ganzel of the Boston Beaneaters and Holy Cross's Tim Murnane joined Hart, Manning, Woods, McCarthy and others in testifying to the beauty of their avocation of choice.

The host surprised one and all with a fireworks display, the night ending with a promise to return for another outing in 1907. Hart vowed to find the old-timers who had not made the trip on that day but stated that "those who have forsaken baseball for golf and lawn tennis aren't wanted at all."

Return they would, for the next several years, the event growing in size and prominence until John Irwin ran afoul of the law for shady dealings at his inn. But as Tim Murnane wrote in *Baseball Magazine* in 1908, a new American tradition had begun. "No other city in the country can boast as Boston does of an Old Timers' Day in baseball," he opined. "It has been such a decided success that there is little doubt the idea will spread all over the country."

1909: "Good-by, Dear Heart, Good-by"

B ernice James fondly remembered the sights and sounds of a Hull Village winter. The town flooded the park behind her 30 Main Street home when temperatures dropped low enough to freeze water into ice, and skaters took to it with the joyous laughter that accompanied those first few strides on wobbly ankles and unsteady skates. Steamship whistles at Pemberton, the western tip of the peninsula, faded away in early fall, and the trains of the railroad line that reached the tip the year after she was born rarely rolled into town in the winter months. The coldest months, occasionally interrupted by a harsh seasonal storm, were the most peaceful time of the year in the sleepy little town.

Bernice's friends and neighbors, though, for a few years associated one other beautiful sound with a Hull Village winter. During those early years of her life, Bernice's vocal talents became quite obvious. The Hull Jameses had always taken their music seriously. Bernice's great-grandfather, William James, had soloed in Boston on the clarinet, and future generations even formed "James Family Orchestras," with male and female ensembles. At age eight, she left to study opera in New York at the National Conservatory under the "maker of artists," Oscar Saenger. Eight years later, at sixteen, she became an instructor at the school, where another teacher, Salvatore Mangione de Pasquale, had "become attentive to her." They were married that year.

At twenty years old, the young coloratura soprano got her big break. While traveling in Milan with her husband, she sought work with the local opera companies, but there were simply no spots available. As they discussed possibilities with an agent, his telephone rang; one of the companies was in emergency need of a soprano. Bernice auditioned and beat out twenty-four others for the job in *Rigoletto* at the Del Verme Theater. The musical James family genes proved viable even in the Old World, and her pleasant features helped outclass the competition. "Her father, William James," *Hull Beacon* editor Floretta Vining explained to *Putnam's Magazine*, "is as good-looking a man as you would see anywhere." She shined that night as Gilda.

Bernice DePasquale of Hull sang with Enrico Caruso at the Metropolitan Opera House. *Courtesy of Hull Historical Society.*

With that chance performance, her career took off. She sang in South Africa, Greece, Mexico, Cuba, Berlin, London and Paris. In 1908, Vining sponsored a dinner for the couple at the Pemberton House hotel in Hull, "one of the most notable receptions in the history of this town," according to the *Boston Globe*. In 1909, Bernice made her American debut, replacing Marcella Sembrich as Susanna in a performance of *Le Nozze di Figaro* at the Metropolitan Opera House. Conductor Gustav Mahler had given her just eight days to prepare for the role. Following her performance, Mahler vigorously shook her hand, declaring, "Madam, you are wonderful!" The audience called her out for one curtain call after another, according to William M. "Doc" Bergan's *Old Nantasket*, until she had graced them twenty-six times. One reviewer, though, Henry Charles Lahee, claimed that she was not such an instant success, saying that "though her stage presence was attractive and she made excellent use of the few dramatic possibilities offered by the work, she was nervous and did not do herself justice. The audience was sympathetic." She continued to work hard, often pushing herself beyond healthful bounds and even fainting twice during a December 1909 performance of *Marta*.

By 1912, though, she had certainly perfected her craft. "Mme. de Pasquali's [sic] work commended itself highly to connoisseurs when she first appeared at this house a few years ago, and she has grown to be a far greater and more finished artist in the meanwhile," stated one reviewer. "Both vocally and dramatically Mme. de Pasquali has improved greatly since she was last heard here. Her tones were very beautiful—particularly in the upper register, where they were of limpid purity—and she demonstrated conclusively that emotional coloring of the voice is not necessarily incompatible with coloratura singing." She remained with the Met as the lead soprano trough 1917.

Throughout her professional life, Bernice never forgot her beloved hometown. Though she left it at such a young age, she still felt compelled to return whenever she could during the winter holidays, singing "Silent Night" and other selections in Elm Square in Hull Village, in front of today's Hull Public Library, itself dedicated in 1913.

Tragically, Bernice lost Salvatore in 1923, by which time her star had already begun to fade. She died two years later in 1925, overexerting herself on a stage in Omaha, Nebraska, while suffering from pleurisy, despite her doctor's admonition against extending her tour with a vaudeville company.

Buried in Hull, her tombstone, overlooking Hull Bay, bears the words written by her grieving mother, Eliza Ann: "With deepest sorrow we mourn and cry. Until we meet again, good-by, dear heart, good-by."

1909: For People Who Like to "Do Things"

C entennials are obvious moments for reflection. Although few of us actually live to see the beginning and end of a one-hundred-year cycle, we do have opportunities to celebrate the continuation of the work of someone who preceded us in our passions. The folks at the Jones River Village Historical Society in Kingston did just that all throughout 2009.

The Jones River Village Historical Society, in name, has only been around since 1973, but its predecessor, the Jones River Village Club, has been doing good work since 1909. History was just one focus of the club's early efforts. But the efforts, not the focus, were the key. The time called for men and women of action, people dedicated to making the town a better place in the wake of the waning shipbuilding business, the rise of the automobile and other factors transferring public attention from the community. Put simply by one of the busiest women in Kingston, Emily Fuller Drew, the effort was there. "The club did things," she said.

Like many civic-minded groups of the time, the Jones River Village Club, named for the village named for the river named for the captain of the *Mayflower*, spread out its philanthropy and volunteer energy. It started with five standing committees: conservation of resources, cultivation of land, village improvement, education and history. Each left its mark on the town, through tree plantings, public park clean-ups, free lectures and more. For example, "A large tract of burnt land, land ravaged by fire after fire until its natural goodness was almost spent, was purchased by the club, through subscription," wrote Emily Drew, "and presented to the state for

Visits to the Major John Bradford House in Kingston can come with breakfast and tours of the house and gardens. *Courtesy of the author.*

reforestation. Ponds and streams were stocked with fish, the 'herring laws' were enforced and the former wealth of the brooks brought back through the efforts of the club."

But the signature moment in the history of the club came in 1921. While the formation of the Kingston Grange in 1913 diverted the club's attention away from many of its goals, as the new organization picked up the work, Drew and her cohorts, notably Sarah DeNormandie Bailey, Helen Holmes and Sally Dawes Chase, staked out the ancient Major John Bradford Homestead on Landing Road. They waited for their chance to purchase it and did so for $2,000 from owner Ezra Wright in February of that year, financed by Drew. The club finally had a home.

More than just a home, though, the Bradford House became a beloved gathering spot, a place where breakfasts were served on summer Sundays in the open air as tour guides rang handbells to announce the next guided walk through history. A place where one could wander through Mary's Garden and understand the value kitchen gardens had to early settlers. A place where each fall, the word "harvest" still meant what it originally meant to the Bradfords.

Behind the scenes, though, there's always been much more going on than meets the eye of the casual visitor. In the early 1970s, the grounds were opened up by an archaeology crew. Pipe stems and bowls, bottles, dishes and broken pottery shards have helped to detail the story of the house, especially in conjunction with the results of a dendrochronology study accomplished three decades later. An early twenty-first-century conditions assessment accomplished with Community Preservation grant money gave the society a road map for the future preservation needs of the home. There are urgent needs and preventative measures that could be taken. As with all homes, doors, windows, shingles and gutters all need to be replaced at some time.

In the meantime, the society continues to reach out to the public through education programs, keeping true to the intentions of the original club members. Third graders from the local elementary school annually contribute artwork for a summer-long exhibition in the barn, itself a recent addition to the grounds, having been purchased in West Bridgewater, torn down piece by numbered piece and rebuilt on site in 2003.

Perhaps, though, the best years are yet to come for the Jones River Village Historical Society. The club reinvigorated its ranks around the time of the tercentennial celebration of the pilgrims' landing at Plymouth in 1620, giving that final push to purchase the Bradford House for preservation. In 2009, the quadricentennial celebration was just more than a decade away. For all of the Pilgrim-related historic sites on the South Shore, a major influx of visitors, if even just a portion of the tens of millions of *Mayflower* descendants chose to make the journey, will descend on the area in years to come. Those folks tracing their routes back to the Bradford family will be very happy by what they see, thanks to the efforts of a positive group of people who still, one hundred years later, like to "do things."

1909: War Games

It had already been quite an exciting year. In January, British explorer Ernest Shackleton and his expedition located the magnetic South Pole. Just a few months later, Robert Peary and Matthew Henson found what they believed was the North Pole. Ex-president Theodore Roosevelt, freshly out of office, headed to Africa on behalf of the Smithsonian Institution and the National Geographic Society in March, the same month that the White Star Line laid down the keel of what it hoped would be its most successful transatlantic passenger liner of all time, a mammoth vessel it called *Titanic*.

Closer to the South Shore, on June 22, financier August Belmont proudly watched as work began on his most ambitious project to date, the excavation of a waterway from Massachusetts Bay to Buzzards Bay, what he called the Cape Cod Canal.

No one on the South Shore, though, was prepared for the headline that screamed across the front page of the *Rockland Standard* on July 16, 1909. War was coming back to Plymouth County.

"Troops May Invade Town," the headline read, "Rockland Maidens Preparing to Entertain." In an effort to give the state militia some much-needed combat experience, Massachusetts had agreed to be "invaded" by the militias of New York, Connecticut, New Jersey and the District of Columbia during the week of August 14 to 21. It's difficult to tell, a century removed from the exercise, who was most excited—the local shopkeepers or the local ladies.

1909

Gov. Draper,
Abington - Aug. 19, 1909.

Governor Eben Draper attended the war games that ran through Hanover, Abington and other South Shore towns. *Courtesy of Historical Society of Old Abington.*

"We shall have to buy a good deal of wood, forage, etc.," wrote William H. Bingham of the Massachusetts Adjutant General's Office to the Rockland selectmen, "and no doubt the troops will leave a good deal of money in the territory in which they operate." The *Rockland Standard*, on the other hand, reported, "Much interest is being taken in the coming maneuvers, especially by the young maidens of the various towns about this part of the state. As a result, the dressmakers are being rushed with orders so that the ladies may appear at their best should the troops happen to visit them." Either way, the local economy won.

The war games plan called for the "enemy" troops to try to invade Massachusetts from the south and fight their way to Boston, while everyday life rumbled along around the conflict. The state's adjutant general promised that officials would survey the battlefields after the maneuvers had ended and would "estimate any possible damages to fences, walls, etc., and pay cash as soon as an agreement is reached."

The combined alien forces struck with mock fury into the defensive line set up by the Massachusetts boys from Plymouth to Rhode Island. Outstanding tactical maneuvering by the invaders set them free on a straight course toward Boston, but the Massachusetts force caught them from behind, engaging them in a pitched battle at Hanover Four Corners and over the North River Bridge. Hanover historian Barbara Barker picks up the story:

> *One of the largest encampments was located in the Sylvester fields, near the present Cardinal Cushing School* [in Hanover]. *Many of the men were farmers, factory workers, shop keepers, and the like and were unused to the rugged terrain and work. Some were called "tenderfoots." Some got lost as they charged the enemy through the swampy areas, and didn't find their way out for two days. Many such exhausted were carried out on stretchers. Many begged food from the country folk because their camp was miles away. Some wells in Hanover went dry because of the demand for water.*
>
> *The men trampled fields like cattle as they charged the enemy. The heaviest cannon fire occurred on the last day, when the two forces met on a nearby site. The detonation of the cannons, which was set off on Broadway, broke dishes from shelves in neighboring kitchens and broke every pane of glass in Herman Sturtevant's house.*

When the invaders failed to take the North River Bridge, they fell back, giving the field—and the "war"—to the boys from Massachusetts.

Over the next couple of days, the troops spared Rockland but marched through Abington, up Washington Street and past the Abington Savings Bank building, the conquering heroes of a bloodless war. A magnificent painting of the army hangs today in the Dyer Memorial Library in Abington.

Over in Rockland, the young maidens who had hoped beyond hope that their princes were on the way, returned disappointedly to their daily lives, and the local Romeos breathed a sigh of relief.

1909: Boss

U p until 1909, he was just John Smith. For a while, he was patrolman
John Smith, when he worked for the Hull Police Department. And in
1893, he became selectman John Smith. It wasn't until 1909, though, that
he became Boss John Smith.

In the fall of that year, the town of Hull was primed to exercise its agreed-
upon right to send a local man to the state's House of Representatives from the
local district. The openly discussed agreement forged years in the past stated
that Hull would send its local man to the house every ten years, with Hingham
and Cohasset—with much larger populations—filling the interim seats.

Yet the process of choosing one Hull man for the job did not necessarily
go smoothly every time it came around. The candidate for 1909, of course,
would be a Republican, as since 1900, the Republican Town Committee had
held full control of Hull's political present and future. The question came
down to which Republican candidate would be nominated to trounce the
local Democratic candidate and head for Beacon Hill. Clarence Nickerson,
town treasurer and head schoolteacher, had the backing of John Smith, and
Richard B. Hayes, a lawyer, did not, as they headed for the 1909 caucus.

Smith wrote an open letter to the voters of Hull through the August 27,
1909 *Hull Beacon*. He referred to the 1899 election and discord at the polls and
the need for solidarity behind the right candidate. And the right candidate,
he said, was Nickerson, who, coincidentally, was married to Smith's niece.
The Hayes camp fired back in the newspaper the following week: "He
[Hayes] is a life-long Republican who has always supported the candidate

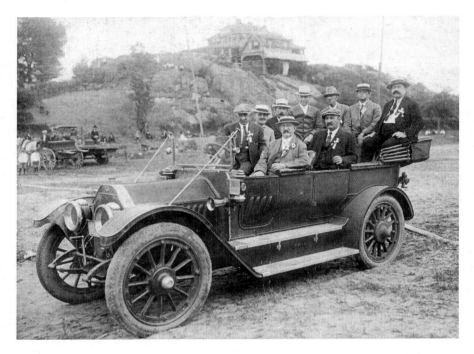

John Smith (back row, center) ran Hull like a well-oiled machine. *Courtesy of Hull Historical Society.*

of his party faithfully and loyally. Mr. Hayes has never been mixed up in any local factional contests," the writer said, referring to Smith's implications. Talk on the streets on September 17 said that Hayes was gaining strength in the days leading up to the caucus. Even the local temperance advocates stood behind him, threatening to run their own candidate if Nickerson was selected at the caucus.

The attacks on Smith and Nickerson did not end there. A letter signed by a "Citizen of Hull" debated whether or not Nickerson could balance the town's priorities if elected and whether or not Smith had the right to let that happen. "If the political boss can take a teacher away from his school, send him to the legislature and hold the place of teacher for him indefinitely, then it is about time that there should be a change in teachers and bosses," he wrote.

And so "Boss" Smith was born.

John Smith took all of the attacks in stride. After all, as William M. "Doc" Bergan stated in *Old Nantasket*, "The Old Ring could support a wild baboon in a cage against a clergyman of the Gospel and the gentleman of the cloth would surely go down to ignominious defeat." Nickerson won, and Smith feted him at George Smith's Tavern, "where they sat down to a feast such as Lucullus never knew. The two candidates for the honor, Clarence V. Nickerson, who was successful, and Richard B. Hayes, who gave the victor such a close run, sat at the head of the table. All their differences were amicably settled, and the banquet was in the nature of a love feast." It was, in fact, a last supper for Hayes. He and his family moved out of town that week.

What came next can only be described, at the least, as odd, at the most, shadowy. John Smith had demonstrated in the past that he could convince Republicans to vote Democrat when it suited the town's needs. But in this instance, he professed to do just the opposite, to sway the fifty-five or so Democrats in town to vote Republican and vault Nickerson to victory.

With only 282 voters taking part in the elections in Hull (the population had barely broken 1,000 in 1900), statistical analysis of the results was a simple game. The town voted, as expected, overwhelmingly Republican in all contests. Yet though they had consistently cast between 156 and 164 votes in all of the other contested races excluding governor and lieutenant governor, Nickerson drew 252 of the 282 votes cast for representative. The Democrats, who posted between 45 and 53 votes for their candidates, cast only 19 for George A. Cole of Hingham. The third candidate, Harold G. Leavitt of Hingham, of the supposedly mighty and threatening Prohibition Party, received 5 votes. And where there had been a consistent 61 to 69 blanks through the rest of the contests, the battle for representative polled only 6 blank ballots. John Smith had not only convinced the local Democrats to vote Republican, he somehow persuaded approximately 56 men who otherwise did not vote in any contest other than governor and lieutenant governor to help him elect Clarence V. Nickerson.

Cole took two of the three towns, capturing 51 percent of the Hingham vote and 62 percent of the Cohasset vote. Yet in Hull, his measly 19 votes totaled less than 7 percent of the number cast, a dramatic drop from the rest of the results. Taking the mean averages of the other Hull elections—a 30 Democrat-Republican vote swing, and a 59 vote change from blanks to Republican for representative—results showed a difference of 89 votes in favor of Nickerson that statistically should not have been there. Of the 1,507 votes cast, Nickerson boasted 763 and Cole 690. Had those 89 votes not mysteriously swung his way in Hull, Nickerson would have been soundly defeated. Instead, he was on his way to Beacon Hill, thanks to Boss John Smith.

1909: A Season of Storms

Not since the great storm when the *Portland* was lost has Nantasket and Hull experienced such a storm," Floretta Vining wrote in her December 3, 1909 *Hull Beacon* editorial, "Thanksgiving Eve Storm." Delayed by broken tracks at South Station in Boston and expecting to be home at the six o'clock hour, Vining found herself struggling against the wind and more close to ten o'clock. With the tracks disrupted beyond the Stony Beach crossing near the end of the peninsula, "each and every one of us landed in a raging sea to walk along the highway" and "every one of us got a drenching never to be forgotten. One does not care to bathe in the Ocean on Nov. 24th."

The tides scoured the beaches, causing ruts and gullies to form. Cotton cloth from the 1904 wreck of the *Belle J. Neale* washed ashore by the bolt-load. "No houses were taken off their foundations to my knowledge as they were at Scituate about the sand hills," wrote Vining. "The sea still continues to roar and cast up large waves; it really is a great sight to see the foam from the angry waves. I hope we won't have another such storm this winter."

As usual with a late fall or early winter nor'easter, the people of Hull enjoyed both good and bad aftereffects. While summer residents flocked to the shore to ascertain the damage to their cottages, those folks who had lived in town for a long time knew the sea had more to offer than the soggy bolts of cloth now hanging out to dry in backyards around the village. "The long beach was strewn with the large clams which can only be found at extreme low tide. Many a good chowder the residents of Hull have had this week."

The schooner *Nantasket* was a casualty of the early winter storms of 1909. *Courtesy of Scituate Historical Society.*

The town sent an army of men out to clean up the railroad tracks and repair the line at Stony Beach.

For a while, the weather returned to its early fall splendor. On Christmas Eve, Vining, who believed with all her heart that Hull temperatures pushed the mercury ten degrees higher than at Boston all winter long, proclaimed, "The weather has been pleasant but cool at Hull and has been so for several years. One can make it here until January and February; these are the only months to go away."

December had something to say about that.

"The greatest storm ever known along the coast is the talk of every one and trying to put things in order keeps everybody busy," opened the December 31 *Hull Beacon*. "Wood by the quantities is being teamed to the homes of the residents.

"The storm on Thanksgiving eve, quite severe in its way, was not to be compared with the one that set in Christmas night," stated Vining in her editorial, "The Christmas Storm." "Saturday was a fairly pleasant day, and it was not until after sunset that there were any pronounced signs of a storm. But along during the night the storm began, and daybreak found the New England coast in the grasp of the storm king."

That Sunday morning's eleven o'clock high tide outraced even the Portland Gale's by at least five feet, according to Captain Louis G. Serovich, who had been out saving lives during that fateful storm in 1898. "At Stony Beach, the tide began to come over the breakwater, across the railroad track, and poured into the low land in a torrent. People living in the vicinity were driven from their homes, and took refuge with their more fortunate neighbors." The recently repaired railroad tracks at Stony Beach washed away entirely, and the station building itself was nearly destroyed. For a full three hours, the braver occupants of the cottages on Stony Beach remained awash in the tide, most huddling in second-floor rooms hoping their homes would withstand the power of the storm.

"The whole waterfront from Pemberton to Green Hill suffered severely," wrote Vining. "Great damage was done on the ocean side from Allerton to Atlantic Hill. Breakwaters were demolished, doors and windows broken in and tons of stone, gravel and driftwood deposited in the rooms and cellars." At Green Hill, the water washed away about twenty feet of the seaside bluffs, undermining the homes standing thereon. "The houses of Charles W. Grove of Hanover and Dr. Charles R. Greeley of South Weymouth are now suspended like Mahomet's coffin, between heaven and earth." At Gun Rock, Civil War veteran and longtime resident Horace E. Sampson and his wife barely escaped with their lives, as several houses fell from their foundations. All along the shore, the flags, masts and streamers of the five-masted schooner *Davis Palmer*, lost on Graves Ledge during the storm, drifted ashore.

When the winds died, the old-timers pulled out their measuring sticks. Forget about the Portland Gale, they all said. "This storm was, without exception, the severest since the storm that carried away Minot's Light in 1851. Old inhabitants of Hull say that while it lasted, it was the worst they ever knew." The only redeeming trait about the storm was the fact that the wind shifted during the day from northeast to northwest, "otherwise the damage caused by the high tide of that night would have been fifty times greater."

As usual, the people of Hull got right to work rebuilding their storm-torn homes and streets. Heads were counted, and handshakes and smiles greeted all the survivors of yet another late-fall disaster. Life went back to normal, but no one could say it had not been one heck of a holiday season.

1910: To the Air

Cromwell Dixon had a grand plan. He would fly his dirigible from Quincy to Boston to hand deliver invitations from the gathered aviators at the first Harvard-Boston Aero Meet at Squantum to Governor Eben S. Draper and Mayor John "HoneyFitz" Fitzgerald. But Dixon had not counted on one thing: heavy east winds. Crowds gathered on rooftops in Boston on September 2, 1910, waited in vain, as Dixon was forced to skip what would have been a fantastic marketing moment for his new flying machine.

The show, though, would go on, and it would open eyes around the world as to the possibilities of heavier-than-air flight. Manned flight had been around since the Montgolfier brothers' balloon drifted over Paris on November 21, 1783, but engine-driven flights were new, exciting and about to drive America crazy with delight.

It had been only seven years since the Wright brothers had lifted off their flying machine at Kitty Hawk, North Carolina, in 1903 and soared for an exhilarating twelve seconds. By 1910, the French had a military air force. It boasted only five planes.

Despite never receiving their invitations from the air, both Draper and Fitzgerald arrived at the meet, sponsored by the Harvard Aeronautical Society and the Aero Club of New England from September 3 to 10. They came to see the stars of the air: Glenn Curtiss, Clifford B. Harmon and the dashing young Englishman Claude Graham-White.

Graham-White had only received his pilot's license—in France—on January 4 but by midsummer had set flight longevity records in Europe,

Left: Cromwell Dixon's dirigible was a star of the first Harvard Aero Meet in Quincy. *Courtesy of Quincy Historical Society.*

Below: Claude Graham-White set the world of the first Harvard Aero Meet afire. *Courtesy of Quincy Historical Society.*

soaring for more than an hour and twenty minutes. On September 3, he took to the skies in his Bleriot monoplane in a test flight for a total of six minutes, reaching speeds up to 60 miles per hour. Although racecars had already topped this speed (Fred Marriott and his Stanley Rocket Racer held the record at 127 miles per hour), as had Charles "Mile-A-Minute" Murphy on his bicycle in 1899, neither had granted the spectacle of man defying gravity and conquering the sky.

That day witnessed three crashes, including one by Graham-White himself. Clifford B. Harmon's plane suddenly lost altitude and dove into the ground, and Ralph Johnstone's motor gave out in separate incidents, both planes crashing without injuries to the pilots. Back on earth, Graham-White and A.V. Roe's automobile struck a telegraph pole, but they, too, were unhurt.

Although plans had called for an opening of the grounds to the public on Sunday, September 5, newly elected Harvard president Abbott Lawrence Lowell declared the meet closed to observe the Sabbath. Despite guards on duty, several people made their way into the field anyway. When Graham-White came out to inspect his planes, he found them covered with graffiti.

On September 6, the spectacle began, and Graham-White quickly ingratiated himself to the crowd. "He appeared first in his dragonfly Bleriot monoplane," read the *New York Times*. "At the very outset, he was spectacular. He took his rise from the lane between the hangars, tearing directly toward the main grandstand, rising into the air and shooting over the heads of the crowd." Exhibitions reigned for part of the day as William H. Willard did the unthinkable and took a woman aloft. Not to be outdone, Graham-White shared his second seat with another. Little did either man know that the first female solo flight would take place that week in Hammondsport, New York, when a plane with a limiter on its throttle accidentally gained enough speed and took Blanche Stuart Scott into the air for forty feet.

Contests began for speed and altitude and landing accuracy, with timed races and head-to-head races as well. The highlight of the week was the long-anticipated race to Boston Light and back. The favorite took up his position, and he did not disappoint his fans. At 4:30 p.m. on September 7, "Graham-White's hand dropped the signal to the mechanicians to free the machine. It rose in the air and whizzed over the starting line at a faster rate than the biplanes have been making. As he passed the grandstand, the spectators broke out in wild cheering." Twenty-five thousand spectators roared as the Englishman took the day.

President William Howard Taft, though, who arrived for the afternoon of September 8, was most interested in one specific contest category: bomb dropping. Flying just three hundred feet above their target, a makeshift battleship laid out in the fields below, the pilots let fly mock bombs by leaning out of their cockpits and letting them go from their hands to the target. He waved and cheered as John Fitzgerald took to the air with Graham-White, amused by the display, but upon seeing the bomb-dropping competition, Taft instructed his new secretary of the Navy, George von Lengerke Meyer of Boston, to study the potential of carrier-based aviation.

Although the concept of military aviation was not born that day in Quincy, its American roots certainly run through the first Harvard-Boston Aero Meet.

1911: Heat Wave

It wasn't as if they hadn't been warned. The people of the South Shore had already felt the power of the sun in May, when a late-month rising of the mercury topped out at ninety degrees. The belief, then, was that no one in the Boston area would see that kind of heat again in 1911. Then came July.

It promised to be warm on July 2 when the sun rose, a comfortable seventy-two degrees at 6:00 a.m. By noon, it had reached ninety-one, and the heat continued well into the night. The *Boston Globe* gave the day its place in history with its July 3 edition:

> *Not since 10 years ago today has Boston experienced such a hot day as yesterday, according to official records of the U.S. observation station, and late last night, forecasters promised absolutely no relief from the torrid wave either today or tomorrow. For the practically unprecedented period of nine hours, the official temperature yesterday remained above 90. For the first time in nearly a score of years, it registered 90 degrees as late as 8 p.m. and at 10 p.m. had descended only to 85.*

Mayor John Fitzgerald ordered the city's ferry boats opened free of charge to all local citizens, allowing them to cool themselves with whatever breezes the motion of the boats could muster. Hundreds went to the city's bridges, where the city had placed benches in hopes of offering respite from the heat. Others escaped to the state bathhouses in Hull, Revere and

The hottest days of summer have always brought the masses to Nantasket Beach. *Courtesy of Hull Historical Society.*

Nantasket Beach attracts all kinds of revelers. *Courtesy of Hull Historical Society.*

Lynn, while still others just gave in. Heat prostration cases headlined the newspapers. Thomas Owens of South Boston took his own life, rather than cope with the heat, leaping from his second-story window to his death.

Quincy beaches rung with the greatest activity seen in years. Workmen frantically completed construction of a new women's bathhouse on the Town River. "Steamboats, electrics and trains carried thousands to the beaches, while automobiles scurried over the roads in every direction carrying a great many more in search of temporary relief," reported the *Globe*. Eighty thousand people packed Nantasket Beach.

"Many found relief by plunging into the surf," continued the *Globe*, while others "stuck closely to the sheltering shade of pavilions and verandas." A larger crowd of 125,000 sought relief at Revere Beach and were treated to a rare occurrence as President William Taft rolled through town, waving to the crowd at the bathhouse.

And that was just day one.

On July 3, temperatures rose again, reaching 102 degrees, and on the Fourth of July, thermometers read 104. The *Hull Beacon* estimated 110,000 visitors on Nantasket Beach on Independence Day. "The Northern railroad sent out cars in both directions just as fast as they could be loaded up and it was the same with the steamboats, extra boats were filled the moment they made a landing and returned to Boston immediately," wrote Floretta Vining in her editorial column. "The wharf was packed from the boat to the end of the pier with humanity about 9 o'clock. I never saw anything like it before and not one accident up to date, and no drunks."

Elsewhere, folks were not faring as well. On July 6, the *Boston Globe* ran a listing of twenty-one people, from infants to nonagenarians, who had died from the heat in the city alone. A sub-list compiled the brief stories of dozens of others throughout New England who had succumbed, from Sarah Dolan, found dead in the woods on North Windsor, Maine, to an "Unknown Scotchman" who died in his hospital bed in Springfield. J. Henry Herrick, an undertaker in Hudson, collapsed and died while working on the body of Mary Thornton Wheeler, joining her in the ghoulish statistics of the day. Another undertaker came in to complete the Wheeler job and start on Herrick.

On Wednesday the fifth, the temps dropped to a high of 95 but climbed again on the sixth to 101. Relief, in the form of the high 70s, reigned on Friday and Saturday, but on the ninth, the mercury rose again into the 90s. The second wave drove even more people to the shore, as 200,000 descended on Revere Beach. On July 12, the *Globe*'s death list reached twenty-six in

Boston proper, eighty-five in New England total. Suicides continued. Thirty-year-old Thomas O'Hare of Fall River drank carbolic acid in front of his family, dying within minutes at the feet of his mother and sister. Elsewhere, more sensibility ruled. "A number of people in Hingham were out until 3 o'clock this morning walking around in bathing suits trying to keep cool, and found it impossible to sleep, the heat was so terrific," wrote the *Hingham Bucket* on July 14.

Eventually, it had to break, and it did. But four Boston-area heat records, for July 3, 4, 6 and 11, have stood the test of time, lasting for more than one hundred years.

1912: The Demise of the Thinking Machine

Jacques Futrelle was a man living a dream. In April 1912, the Scituate novelist found himself in Europe, shopping his "Thinking Machine" mysteries to foreign markets, opening up a new world for his fictional detective already being touted as an American Sherlock Holmes.

Futrelle started life in Georgia in 1875, landing a job with the *Atlanta Journal* at just eighteen years old. A run to Massachusetts to work for the *Boston Post* ended quickly, as homesickness sent him back to the *Journal* and into the arms of his sweetheart, Lillie May Peel, whom he married in 1895. Following his passions, he again jumped to the northeast and took a job on the telegraph desk of the *New York Herald*. When the Spanish-American War broke out in 1898, he manned his desk twenty-four hours a day until exhaustion drove him from the work. Needing recuperation, he retreated to his sister-in-law's home in seaside Scituate.

Futrelle spent the next two years in Virginia working in theater. When he reemerged in the newspaper world, it was again in the Bay State, with the *Boston American* in 1904, and it was there that he unleashed his legacy on the world, the character that would make him famous, Professor Augustus S.F.X. Van Dusen, PhD, LLD, FRS, MD, etc., etc.: "The Thinking Machine."

Starting with the serialized and miraculous tale "The Problem of Cell 13," in which Van Dusen, a seemingly self-employed Boston-area logician, accepts the challenge of breaking out of a maximum-security prison, Futrelle sends his egotist on a series of more than forty short mysteries,

Jacques Futrelle's widow is buried in a small cemetery in Scituate. *Courtesy of the author.*

typically accompanied by, perhaps semi-autobiographically, an intrepid young reporter, Hutchinson Hatch.

Futrelle, now living full time in Scituate with May, described Van Dusen in "The Burglar and the Girl." "He was five feet, two inches tall, weighed about 107 pounds, that being slightly above normal, and wore a number eight hat. Bushy, yellow hair straggled down about his ears and practically framed a clean-shaven, wizened face in which were combined the paradoxical qualities of extreme aggressiveness and childish petulance." More important than his looks, though, was his mind. "By his personal efforts, he had mercilessly flattened out and readjusted at least two of the exact sciences and had added immeasurably to the world's sum of knowledge in others." Van Dusen believed that logic, and logic alone, could win almost any human battle. "Two and two make four, not sometimes, but all the time," he often repeated.

In 1906, Futrelle left newspapers for full-time novel writing. Knocking down an old home at Scituate Harbor, he and May had their own built. They called it Stepping Stones. At just thirty-one years old, Futrelle was looking forward to a long career and potentially becoming known as one of the United States' all-time great mystery writers.

Early in 1912, before embarking for Europe, Futrelle visited his mother, Linnie, in Georgia. With his future so bright, he wanted to expand his horizons and expose new parts of the world to his Thinking Machine.

He wrote while in the Old World, planning on expanding his character's adventures when he got home to Scituate. He spent a month in Italy and even visited Scotland Yard.

On April 9, 1912, he and several friends partied well into the night in celebration of Futrelle's thirty-seventh birthday. At 3:00 a.m., he and May decided to skip sleep and began packing for their journey home. As soon as they could, they headed for Southampton.

There, they boarded the *Titanic*.

During the night of the April 14, Jacques Futrelle began suffering from headaches. When the ship struck the iceberg, he assured his wife things would be alright—that no baby berg could ever take down such a large and magnificent vessel. She begged him to investigate. His discoveries let them know that their lives were, indeed, in grave danger.

In the mad scramble that followed that night, Jacques edged May toward collapsible lifeboat D. She returned to him time after time, imploring him to join her. "'For God's sake, go!' he fairly screamed at me as he tried to push me away, and I could see how he suffered," she told the *New York Times* on April 19, 1912. "'It's your last chance, go!' Then one of the ship's officers forced me into a lifeboat, and I gave up all hope that he could be saved.'" When she saw him last, Jacques Futrelle was lighting a cigarette with Colonel John Jacob Astor, warily surveying the ocean. His body was never found. "Jacques is dead," she told the *Times*, "but he died like a hero, that I know."

"Mr. Jacques Futrelle," wrote the *Scituate Light* on Friday, April 26, 1912, "seemed to have a premonition of tragedy before sailing. Mr. Futrelle and his wife took the precaution of sending from London to Mrs. Futrelle's brother John Peel of Atlanta power of attorney for the administration of their estates should anything befall them. He also sent a list of the banking houses where he had his money and securities."

Unable to bear the strain of losing her son, Linnie Futrelle died in July. Stunned by her own loss, May Futrelle tossed a bouquet of flowers into the Atlantic off Scituate every year on the anniversary of *Titanic*'s sinking. She published one final Jacques Futrelle book in 1912, *My Lady's Garter*, dedicating it to "the heroes of the *Titanic*."

1912: First Pitch at Fenway

Organized professional baseball was in its infancy when Thomas O'Brien was born in Brockton in 1882, a city in which most young boys at that time grew up to work in the shoe industry. O'Brien, though, nicknamed "Buck," had something by the beginning of the twentieth century that most young boys didn't. He could throw a spitball that danced in ways that made hitters curse.

It's possible that O'Brien joined the local New England League team, the Brockton Tigers (there later would be a Brockton Shoemakers team) when in his early twenties, but sabermetricians have yet to make the definite connection. We do know, though, that by 1910, he'd caught the eye of Major League scouts. That year, at twenty-eight, O'Brien toed the rubber for the Hartford Senators of the Connecticut State League, leading the league in strikeouts and going twenty wins against ten losses for the season. The Boston Red Sox had seen enough; they purchased his contract from Hartford at the end of the season.

Buck would press westward, though, before making this Red Sox debut. Hoping for just a little more honing of his skills, the Sox sent him to the Denver Grizzlies for the 1911 season. There, in the rarified air, his spitball mesmerized hitters. At the time, spitballs—doctored with saliva or other foreign substances to alter the weight distribution and therefore the flight of the ball—were completely legal. O'Brien, at twenty-nine, led the Western League in strikeouts and winning percentage, coming in second in wins with his 26–7 record. Before the Major League season ended, the Red Sox called him up. Backed in center field by future Hall of Famer Tris Speaker, O'Brien started on September 9 and over the last few weeks of the season went 5–1 with an 0.38 earned run average (allowing less than one run per nine innings, a remarkable statistic). The Sox, playing their home games at the Huntington Avenue Baseball Grounds, finished 78–75, in fourth place in the American League.

As spring training broke in 1912, O'Brien joined the Red Sox as a member of the starting rotation, third in line behind "Smoky" Joe Wood, so called because of the speed of his fastball, and fellow rookie right-hander Hugh Bedient. O'Brien took to the mound in New York against the Highlanders (we now know them as the Yankees) in the second game of a double-header on April 12. "Buck did not shine in his strike-out specialty," read the *New York Times* the next day, "chasing only two of the Yankees back to the bench by the fan route, but he scattered New York's six hits through five different innings and showed splendid control." He wavered in the ninth, causing player-manager Jake Stahl to get a reliever up in the bullpen, but he regained his form and finished the game for a 5–3 victory.

Eight days later, after a few days of wet weather, the Red Sox were back in Boston. O'Brien was again sent to the mound, but not at the Huntington Avenue grounds. Instead, he was the first Red Sox hurler to stand atop the bump at the brand new Fenway Park.

Twenty-seven thousand fans gathered at the ballpark for the Opening Day game. Mayor John F. "HoneyFitz" Fitzgerald, President John F. Kennedy's grandfather, threw out the ceremonial first pitch. "The day was ideal," wrote the *Boston Globe* the next day. "The bright sun brought out the bright colors of the flags and bunting that decorated the big grandstand, and gave the new uniforms of the players a natty look." The ground, though, softened by the rain, was "soft and lumpy," which would lead to a sloppily fielded game. The fans, unable to control their excitement, charged onto the field and had to be restrained behind ropes so the game could proceed. The teams made spur-of-the-moment ground rules; any ball hit into the crowd was an automatic double. The new twenty-five-foot-tall wall in left field would not be a participant in the first game at Fenway Park.

O'Brien took the mound in this whirlwind, knowing that among the crowd was another famous pitcher of the moment, a Boston Brave named Cy Young. He struggled from the start, allowing three runs to the Highlanders in the first inning and two more in the third on four hits, four walks, two beanballs, a wild pitch and a balk. Luckily, his teammates were up to the task. When Olaf Henriksen batted for O'Brien in the fourth inning, taking him out of the game, the Red Sox were down 4–3. They'd come back to win 7–6 in eleven innings.

Buck O'Brien won the World Series with the Red Sox that year but played only two more Major League seasons before calling it a career. But he'll go down in the history books as the Brockton boy who threw the first pitch in anger at Fenway Park.

1913: Thanks to All the Dogs

T hat the town ever had a library in the first place was a near miracle. Hull Village, the little community between the wind-blocking hills at the northern reach of the sandy Nantasket peninsula (Nantasket meaning "the place between the tides"), had been evacuated during the American Revolution in the face of the enemy. As the outpost of Boston Harbor, the little community was particularly vulnerable to attack and plundering. After the war ended, only half the population returned. Until the middle of the next century, the motley group of sailors and wreckers and lifesavers never totaled more than 125 people. Perhaps Hingham was right. Maybe Hull was the "moon village at the end of the earth."

But as the Civil War grew closer, Hull changed. The Industrial Revolution, while it had no direct effect on the town as far as factory construction went, separated economic classes and created leisure time as we know it. And where better to spend that time than along the coast. Hull, Scituate, Marshfield, Plymouth and other towns found new lives as summer resorts. Slowly, Hull's year-round population grew to 450 people by 1890. Town services that were once seen as well beyond the scope of the community suddenly took root, as the tax base expanded to accommodate the growing hundreds of summer visitors. Hull became, statistically, one of the richest towns in Massachusetts.

In the fall of 1913, Lizzie A.R. Knight wrote:

> "A word lightly spoken is like apples in a picture of silver." This saying is
> quite a fitting illustration in the fact that the Hull Library came into being

The first library in Hull was a wheeled cart loaded with books in the Hull Village School. *Courtesy of Hull Historical Society.*

through the chance remark of a school teacher uttered thirty or more years ago. The village school at the time was held in the room now occupied by the town as a hose house [i.e., fire station], and one teacher taught all grades, from ABC to algebra. The remark that it would be a fine thing to have a school library appealed to me at once, and I determined it should be brought about if possible.

Knight took advantage of a state law that is still in effect today. Massachusetts General Law chapter 140 section 172 states:

Money received by a county treasurer under the preceding sections relating to dogs, and not paid out for damages, license blanks or books, record books, anti-rabic vaccine or other purposes as required under said sections, shall, in January, be paid back to the treasurers of the towns in proportion to the amounts received from such towns, and the money so refunded shall be expended for the support of public libraries or schools.

The Hull Public Library opened in its permanent home in the former home of poet Jon Boyle O'Reilly. *Courtesy of Hull Historical Society.*

As a member of the school committee, Knight gained the support of her colleagues and hit the streets to get signatures to dedicate the dog tax funds to the library-to-be. The Hull Town Meeting of March 1883 voted to assign the funds for the purchase of books to establish a library. The first monies totaled fifty-four dollars.

The town had so changed by 1887 that it was the summer residents who led the way. Their children held a fair that netted $90 for the library as constituted "a portable book case...placed in care of the teacher in charge of the school." The town appropriated $100 for it in 1896, the first such dedication of town funds. That total doubled to $200 in 1911.

But the town still had no permanent, separate home for the library by that time. With the construction of the Village School in 1888, the town utilized a back room for such purposes, but by 1913, the library held three thousand titles. "Books of adventure, exploration, science, travel, history, biography, etc., have their place," wrote Knight, "as well as those written in lighter vein. For juvenile readers, we have aimed to select books which would inculcate honesty, courage, patriotism, truthfulness, courtesy and kindred virtues that go to the formation of a well-rounded character in boys or girls."

It was time. The Hull Library needed a home, and an amazing opportunity presented itself as a literary landmark went on the market.

Poet John Boyle O'Reilly had come to Hull in the late 1880s after a remarkable life in literature and real-life adventure. He bought and then tore down a historic Cape Cod–style cottage known as the Haswell Estate during the American Revolution and the site of the burial of a British marine lost in battle at Boston Lighthouse. To replace it, he designed and built an ornate summer "cottage" for his family. No sooner was he in the house, it seemed, than he died in it, in 1890.

The house was rented by summer visitors and used as a clubhouse some winters by the locals. Rumors that it was haunted started in 1900. Finally, in 1913, the two roads came together. "It is rumored," editor Floretta Vining of the *Hull Beacon* wrote on January 17, 1913, "that the town has purchased the John Boyle O'Reilly homestead to be used for a library." The purchase would come later, as an act of Town Meeting. "The old John Boyle O'Reilly Homestead on Main street, in Hull village," wrote Vining, "which has been owned by J. Weston Allen of Newton, was bought last week for $3,300 by the town for a public library site. In this house, John Boyle O'Reilly wrote many of his best poems."

And so it has remained in Hull for more than one hundred years, all due to an offhand remark by an overworked teacher, the hard work of an overachieving public servant and people's love for dogs.

1925: Silent Cal Returns

Nobody ever called him garrulous, and he proved that sometimes the best path to success is to remain silent and let the world think what it may of you. Calvin Coolidge lived life that way, and it drove him all the way into the White House.

It was a short road for the Plymouth Notch, Vermont native (the only American president born on the Fourth of July). His road began in January 1916, when he was sworn in as the forty-sixth lieutenant governor of Massachusetts, under Governor Samuel W. McCall. Just seven years later, he would be sworn in again—as the thirtieth president of the United States.

The road to the presidency ran through Hull. That summer of 1916 was one of high politics in the community, but strangely, the presence of the lieutenant governor went mostly unnoticed. He had, though, stiff competition. It wasn't until August 18 that the *Hull Beacon* reported, "Lieut. Governor Calvin Coolidge and family of Northampton are summering on Hull Hill."

James Michael Curley, then mayor of Boston, owned a home on Gallops Hill at the time, although 1916 would prove to be his last summer in the community. He had a penchant for drawing crowds, sending members of his inner circle off to buy fireworks that he would launch from the beach below his house. He delighted in digging for local clams and would indulge the local kids in talk about his favorite professional baseball players, some of whom, like Eppa Jepha Rixey, he chose solely for the melodiousness of their names.

President Calvin Coolidge visited Hull during his term in the Oval Office. *Library of Congress.*

Curley, with deep mob ties, had already been to jail once, and he would go again. He also would become one of the most beloved Boston politicians of all time, propelled by the motto "Curley Gets Things Done." The key was to never ask where the money came from to get those things done.

John "HoneyFitz" Fitzgerald, Curley's bitter political rival and his mayoral predecessor, owned a home at the northwestern base of Allerton Hill. The previous summer had provided a significant moment in the life of his extended family. His daughter, Rose, had given birth to her son, Joseph Kennedy Jr., in a house on Beach Avenue, while HoneyFitz threw a football back and forth with kids on the beach. Joe would grow up to fly and fight in World War II, driven by his father's presidential ambitions for him. Sadly, he would die in a top-secret mission over France when his bomb-laden plane, meant to nose-dive in as a flying bomb, exploded in mid-air.

But HoneyFitz was in his element in Hull in 1916. The town was in the midst of internal turmoil that was tearing apart the fire department. Fires were breaking out up and down the peninsula, keeping the department's engine running to and fro. Eventually, one of the firemen's own properties burned, as did the coal wharf that belonged to the chief. It would all eventually come to a head in a full walkout of the department. One *Hull Beacon* newspaper entry, though, dragged HoneyFitz into the maelstrom after a fire at Paragon Park. "In the morning paper of last Monday, it read that ex-Mayor John F. Fitzgerald had helped the Hull firemen at the Park fire. Let it be known that the Hull firemen have fought fires previous to any help from the ex-mayor and that they are not soliciting his help now in fighting them. Under Chief Mitchell they have a very worthy leader."

In that same edition, the *Hull Beacon* noted, "Lieut-Gov. Calvin Coolidge and family are among the late-stayers on Hull Hill." The following week, the paper noted, "Lieut-Gov. Calvin Coolidge and family have returned to their winter home from the summer colony on the hill." And that was it for the Coolidges in Hull. As America entered World War I in 1917, the lieutenant governor had work to do at his desk and never appeared in the summer colony.

Years later, though, when he was president in 1925, Coolidge made a surprise visit to his old summer home and his old landlord, C.G. Flynn. Heading to address a gathering at the Pemberton Hotel, he ordered the boat carrying him to bypass the steamboat wharf at the end of town and head for the Hull Yacht Club. Paranoid that the president might be lost, the reception committee "dashed in automobiles to the Hull Hill section, where they found, to their amazement, President Coolidge and his wife chatting pleasantly with the Flynns and the Dolans on the piazza of the house where they had enjoyed a summer vacation." The house, still standing on Western Avenue, is still known as Coolidge Cottage.

1926: Red, Red Robin

According to the American Society for Surgery of the Hand, when Harry MacGregor Woods was born with a congenital hand difference in North Chelmsford in 1896, his mother and father probably went through a rapidly changing range of emotions: shock, anger, guilt. They probably wondered about his future.

But baby Harry's parents were hardly the average American mom and dad of the late Victorian age. They both made their livings with their voices. His father, George H. Woods, sang with the Weber Male Quartet of Boston. His mother, Edith MacGregor Woods, traveled with operatic companies. She recalled once being on tour and being given half a day to stand in for a lead who had to sing in Italian. She learned the part phonetically and took the stage, all the while feeling like she was "singing about macaroni and spaghetti." Harry, regardless of the complete lack of fingers on his left hand, would have a wide world of options available to him.

"From earliest childhood, his environment was musical," wrote the *St. Petersburg Evening Independent* in 1930, "so that he thought in terms of music and obtained all the pleasure and happiness from music there was to be had." In 1910, the family moved to Pembroke for the summer, so enjoying their Forest Street home that Edith decided the Woods should remain there permanently. George took a job teaching music in the Abington, Norwell and Pembroke schools. Three years later, the allure of Pembroke as a year-round home waned, and the house became a summer-only abode once again.

Harry attended high school in Pembroke, then Colby Academy in New London, New Hampshire, "became class president, delivered the class speech and wrote the class song, a harbinger of things to come," wrote Paul Salters in Pembroke's tercentennial history, *Pembroke Ancient Trails to the 21ˢᵗ Century, 1712–12012.* "He then entered Harvard College. During summer vacations, he dug clams in Humarock and sold them Sundays at the Quaker Meetinghouse in North Pembroke to help pay his way through Harvard. He also sold fruit and vegetables gathered from trips to Cape Cod from the back of his Ford truck in Duxbury, Marshfield and Brant

Harry MacGregor Woods of Pembroke let the South Shore inspire him. *Courtesy of Pembroke Historical Society.*

Rock to earn pocket money for school." His dance band played gigs at Odd Fellows Hall in Hanover's Four Corners, and audiences praised his piano playing at Bryantville's Mayflower Grove amusement area.

But bigger things were on the horizon.

Harry headed south for New York City's Tin Pan Alley to attempt to forge a life in popular music. His first hit came in 1923, appropriately titled "I'm Goin' South." None other than the biggest star of the day, Al Jolson, sang it right to number two on the charts the following year. In 1925, his "Paddlin' Madeleine Home" hit number three.

Success would come and go fleetingly over the first few years, often due to forces beyond his control, like publishers making bad investment decisions. At those times, or when songwriter's block hit, he returned to Pembroke. In 1926, a glimpse outside a Forest Street window led to "When the Red, Red Robin Comes Bob-Bob-Bobbin' Along," which Jolson took to number one. Down on his luck and his money a year later, Harry returned home to work the cranberry bogs. Clear of mind, he again took off to New York, with a tune in his head that soon backed Mort Dixon's lyrics for "I'm Looking Over a Four-Leaf Clover." The song flopped, only to be revived in 1948 as a major hit.

"Many of his songs, including 'Red, Red Robin,' his mother relates," wrote the *Evening Standard*, "were written at the family homestead, an old farmhouse near West Duxbury on Cape Cod." (Many historical sources list him as a Cape Cod resident; the source of the confusion may be that he lived in a Cape Cod–style home, often described as a "Cape Cod farmhouse.") The songs, American standards, kept coming for the next decade and a half, including "Side by Side," "Try a Little Tenderness" and "Heigh-Ho, Everybody, Heigh-Ho."

Perhaps overcompensating for his deformity, Harry prided himself "on his ability as a golfer, tennis player and swimmer," wrote *The Billboard* on February 24, 1951. "When he had a summer home in the Catskills, he would walk into a Broadway bar and challenge anyone to a wrestling match or other rough-and-tumble feats of strength in which backwoodsmen engage." Bar fights were not beyond his personal bounds.

Eventually, the lure of film brought Harry to Hollywood. He retired to Arizona in 1945 after serving in the U.S. Coast Guard Auxiliary in World War II. He performed for American troops in that war, as well as in Korea and Vietnam. After he died in 1970, he was enshrined in the Songwriters Hall of Fame. In 1987, Pembroke dedicated a memorial bandstand in his honor on the town green.

Harry's sister Dorothy remembered in the *Silver Lake News* that, "He was sitting right here at this table, and he looked out the window and saw a bunch of robins. He said, 'You know, old fellas, you never knew what you did for me.'"

1927: Queen of the Air

A melia Earhart was not born to fly. When first presented with the opportunity as a ten-year-old in 1908, she backed away from a plane—"a thing of rusty wire and wood"—at the Iowa State Fair and asked her father to take her to the merry-go-round instead. It took nearly a decade from that point for the lure of the air to grab hold of her.

In the meantime, Amelia grew up, and unlike the discovery of her love of aviation, that process sadly happened very quickly. Her alcoholic father jumped from railroad job to railroad job and state to state, leaving Amelia and her younger sister to live with their grandparents in Atchison, Kansas. When her grandmother died, Amelia declared the innocence of her childhood over. She had always been a dreamer, keeping a scrapbook of the stories of self-made men and women, hoping to someday find her own path. When the time came to start high school, she went on a search for the best science program in Chicago, there because her father had lost yet another job and the family had found an emergency place to live with friends. She took up nursing, spending considerable time in World War I in Toronto, mending returning soldiers and battling cases of Spanish Influenza. There she came down with a sinus problem that would bother her for the rest of her life. There, too, fate finally had its way.

On a trip to the Canadian National Exposition with a friend, Amelia stood her ground as an exhibition pilot dove at them. She knew that as the moment when the winged beast within her had awoken. In 1919, Amelia enrolled at Columbia University to further her medical studies but dropped

Harold Dennison's hangars attracted the "Queen of the Air," Amelia Earhart. *Courtesy of Quincy Historical Society.*

out after only a year to rejoin her family. Her parents, previously estranged, had reunited in Long Beach, California. On December 28, 1920, a ride with pilot Frank Hawks solidified her future. She began taking lessons—and breaking records. By the time she received her pilot's license on May 15, 1923, only the sixteenth granted to a woman, she had taken her Kinner Airster, which she called "The Canary," to fourteen thousand feet. No woman had ever flown so high.

Family financial setbacks grounded Amelia for several years. Upon her parents' divorce in 1924, she drove her mother cross-country in her convertible, "The Yellow Peril," ending up in Boston. Landing a job as a social worker in Medford, and following several painful operations to repair her sinus problems, she crept back toward a career as a flyer.

On September 3, 1927, Amelia flew aboard the first plane flying out of the new Dennison Airport in Quincy. The airfield, at the corner of Victory Road and East Squantum Street, opened just four months after Charles Lindbergh's pioneering transatlantic flight, but the site already had aviation history in its own past. The Harvard-Boston Aero Meet held at Squantum in September 1910 featured Glenn Curtiss, the Wright Brothers and a dashing young Englishman named Claude Grahame-White. Unfortunately, the 1912 edition of the meet led to the public death of Harriet Quimby, the first woman to fly across the English Channel, when she and her passenger, Will Willard, tumbled one thousand feet to their deaths during an exhibition flight. In 1923, Lieutenant (later Admiral) Richard Byrd opened the navy's first seaplane base at Squantum. Harold Dennison, a trainee at the base, nearly perished in an accident in October of that year. When he opened his flight school and airfield in 1927, with the financial backing of stakeholder Amelia, he stressed safety above all other themes.

For a full year, Amelia devoted her spare time to the airport. When not aiding immigrant mothers with the basics of American life in Medford, she was loading the Yellow Peril with their children for visits to the field to watch flyers in their planes. She acted as a sales rep for Kinner planes, wrote newspaper columns about the joys of flying and continued to log hours in the sky.

Then, suddenly, the call came, the one that she had been waiting for since she was a little girl. A sponsor was looking for a woman to replicate Lindbergh's flight. Amelia jumped at the chance and flew into the history books. On the way from Boston to Newfoundland, from whence the trip would commence, Amelia and her cohorts, Wilmer Stultz and Louis Gordon, dipped their wings over Dennison Airport, waving goodbye to her friends. Her travels nearly took her around the world.

For eight years, Amelia Earhart stood at the head of women's aviation in America, setting speed and height records, including the women's height record in an autogyro. Then, tragically, on July 2, 1937, Amelia and her plane disappeared over the Pacific on an attempted circumnavigation of the earth. After an exhaustive and unsuccessful search, she was declared dead on January 5, 1939. With heavy hearts, her friends at Dennison Airport, in concert with millions around the world, hung their heads in sorrow and remembrance of the "Queen of the Air."

1928: Powerless

The idea of placing a lifeboat onshore that could be used by volunteer rowers to save distressed ships' crews during times of emergency can be traced back to medieval Portugal. In America, the first boat secured for that purpose was located in Cohasset, in 1807. The first American motorized lifeboat was tested in Marquette, Michigan, in 1899, and such boats were in widespread use by the United States Life-Saving Service around the country within ten years of that time.

So why, then, did William Cashman, Edward Stark and Frank Griswold have to die in the employ of their country in a wooden rowboat in 1928?

That year, nearly three decades after the invention of the motorized lifeboat, Boatswain's Mate Cashman and Surfmen Griswold and Stark worked at the U.S. Coast Guard's Manomet Point (Plymouth) station. The station, built in 1904 to replace an earlier building the crew later used exclusively as a boathouse, overlooked the approach to the Cape Cod Canal to the south-southeast and the entrance to Plymouth Harbor to the northwest. The Life-Saving Service had merged with the Revenue Cutter Service in 1915 to form the Coast Guard, just one year after the opening of the Cape Cod Canal.

The opening of the canal had meant an increase in vessel traffic passing into and out of the waters of the southern end of Cape Cod Bay, so much so that the Coast Guard opened an auxiliary station at the eastern end of the canal in 1919. Rounding the bend to the northwest, heading up the coast, mariners looked for the Gurnet Lighthouse at the

The *Robert E. Lee* stranded on Mary Ann Rocks off Manomet, but some passengers didn't even notice. *Courtesy of Old Colony Club of Plymouth.*

The disaster of the *Robert E. Lee* concerned not the shipwrecked crew but the lifesavers who launched to save them. *Courtesy of Old Colony Club of Plymouth.*

end of Duxbury Beach to guide them clear of the offshore, treacherous Mary Ann Rocks.

On the evening of March 9, 1928, Cashman and his crew watched as the four-hundred-foot passenger steamer *Robert E. Lee* headed out of the canal. A blinding snowstorm had terminally shrouded the Gurnet Lighthouse's Fresnel lens seven miles away, hindering Captain Harland W. Robinson's navigational abilities. Snow, sleet and hail entered his wheelhouse as well, driven by forty-five-mile-per-hour winds, adding to the discomfort of the situation. Before he knew what had happened, Cashman's ship had run aground on the rocks. He sent out an SOS call, and fear built as the 2:00 a.m. high tide approached.

Ashore, the Manomet Point crew tried for an hour to contact the ship with flashing lights. Receiving no response, they attempted to launch a wooden rowing lifeboat into the pounding surf, sworn to the Coast Guardsman's unofficial motto, "You have to go out, you don't have to go back." Rebuffed repeatedly by Poseidon's wrath, they opted to wait until first light.

As dawn broke on March 10, many of the 273 passengers on the *Lee* arose to find out for the first time what had happened. One man walked to the shipboard barbershop, completely unaware of the ship's predicament. The stranding had been so gentle that many folks had slept through it all. The SOS call, though, had alerted the Coast Guard cutters *Paulding*, *Active* and *Tuscarora*; the patrol boat *CG-176*; and two thirty-six-foot motor lifeboats, one each from the canal station and from Provincetown's Wood End station, all of which had arrived on scene during the night.

Still unclear as to the ship's true situation, Boatswain's Mate Cashman, Surfmen Stark, Griswold, Alden Proctor, Irving Wood and Joseph Ducharme and volunteer Ernest Douglas finally launched their lifeboat into the bay, headed for the *Robert E. Lee*. Arriving on scene, they found that the situation was under control, with the passengers being ferried to the cutters by the motor lifeboats. As the first passengers transferred, around 11:00 a.m., the Manomet Point crew turned and rowed for home.

As the men neared the shore, a wave estimated by onlookers at twenty-five feet in height picked up the lifeboat's stern. The boat's bow lodged in the sea floor, and the lifeboat pitch-poled, flipping over lengthwise and crashing down on the seven Coast Guardsmen, who floated in the water, stunned. Local men scrambled for whatever boats might be on hand, entering the water in dories and grabbing all but Griswold, who had sunk beneath the surface. Dr. Edgar Hill and Fire Chief Albert Hiller worked on the body of the unconscious William Cashman for a little more than two hours, finally pronouncing him dead. Edward Stark died in transit to Jordan Hospital. Frank Griswold washed ashore the following day. All of the others survived.

Today, a monument stands to the memory of Cashman, Stark and Griswold on Manomet Point, a reminder of the fact that in an age when powered lifeboats were in widespread use around the United States, three members of the Coast Guard's crew at Manomet Point had been left powerless to save their own lives.

1929: Hank Gowdy Touches Them All

With great achievement comes great expectation. Rockland once boasted some of the most important, busiest and recognizable shoe factories in America: Emerson Shoe, Hurley Brothers and E.T. Wright & Company, makers of the "Just Wright Shoe." Skilled laborers who specialized in leather cutting and the other tricks of the shoe trade flocked to the region. But big shoe contracts drove the business. When there were no major orders to fill, entire factories reverted to skeleton crews.

Out of work, Rockland's skilled laborers struggled to provide their families with even the most basic necessities of life. Charitable, civic-minded souls found ways to help by creating repositories for donations to be spent in support of those in need. Such were the state of affairs in Rockland that led to the birth of the Milk Fund for the town's down-on-their-luck schoolchildren.

But Rockland thought big. Knocking on doors and holding public rallies were one thing, but where was the real star power? During the summer of 1929, Frank Jones and "Stubby" Mahon, Rockland do-gooders, spearheaded an effort to utilize one of the town's newest public facilities, the baseball field built in commemoration of the veterans of the recently ended World War I, to raise some serious funds for the youngsters. They reached out to the city of Boston and dared to ask one question: "Would a Major League baseball team consent to playing a game in Rockland and donating the proceeds from the gate to the Milk Fund?"

And so the Boston Braves came to Rockland.

Hank Gowdy of the Boston Braves put on a show when he played in the Rockland Milk Fund game. *Courtesy of National Baseball Hall of Fame.*

The scene was set for Monday night, August 26 at 5:45 p.m. Without lighting at Memorial Park, the organizers wanted to be sure to get in a full nine innings. Pulling out all the stops, Jones and Mahon lined up the Cape Cod League's Falmouth team (later to be known as the Commodores) as opponents.

The town responded with spirit, draping all the buildings of the Union Street business district with bunting and flags in anticipation of the arrival of the teams. Local citizens volunteered to drive to Boston to pick the players up and bring them down to town. After a visit to the Plymouth Rock Ice Cream Company plant in Abington, Judge Emil Fuchs, owner-manager of the Braves that year, and his team were paraded up Union Street to cheering crowds and then headed to the high school gym to prepare for the game.

Thousands packed the stadium and overflowed down the foul lines as their baseball heroes appeared one by one: third baseman Lester Bell, first baseman George Sisler and hero of the 1914 World Series, catcher Hank Gowdy. As the game played out, fans joined the Braves on their bench, forcing many of the players to sit on the ground when their team was at bat.

Gowdy stole the show. With the Braves down early, as pitcher Red Peery gave up four runs in the first two innings, the "old war horse," as the *Rockland Standard* later described him, led off the inning to exaltations from the crowd. "When he came to bat in the third inning, he put his hand to the visor of his cap and looked away into the distance as though he was looking for a good place to send the ball. And then he went and did it," said the *Standard*. With a mighty swing, he slammed a ball to deep left, up and over the wall, to put the Braves aboard. He rounded third "puffing like a porpoise," saying, "My, that's a long way round those bases," with a twinkle in his eye and a smile on his face.

The Braves added three runs in the fourth and four more in the fifth, including a mammoth "Babe Ruth" to center field by Bell, estimated at that time to be the longest ball ever hit at Memorial Park.

In between innings, C.O. Davis stood at a microphone behind home plate and carried on a game-long auction for a single bottle of milk, reminding everyone of why the game was being played. When the sun finally went down and the game was called (the Braves pulled it out, 8–7), Elwin T. Wright, owner of the E.T. Wright Shoe Company, had earned the right to take the bottle home, shelling out an even $100 for the privilege. To sweeten the pot, Judge Fuchs produced a bag of baseballs to be signed by his players and auctioned off. In total, the day's gate and auction items brought in $1,500 for milk for undernourished schoolchildren.

In just two months' time, the Milk Fund would become a subject of even greater importance for the youngsters of Rockland. The onset of the Great Depression after the stock market crash of October 1929 would hit the community hard, as it did the rest of the country. Rockland, though, had found an ally in the Boston Braves and forged a partnership that continued for the next five years, until such a time when the Braves themselves could no longer financially afford to make the trip to town. But no one in Rockland would ever forget the excitement generated the first time a Major League baseball team played in their hometown.

1937: Cookies

R uth Wakefield ran a tight ship. Tighter than most, in fact. "She was as tight as bark on a tree," said one former waitress who worked for her at the Toll House Inn in Whitman.

Wakefield, born in 1903, never intended to get into the restaurant business. Graduating from the Framingham State Normal School Department of Household Arts in 1924, she entered the American workforce as a dietitian. But six years later, she and her husband, Kenneth, purchased the old Smith house on Bedford Street, partially constructed by Jacob Bates in 1816 and 1817 and finished later that year by Lebbeus Smith and his new wife, Jacob's sister Polly. In those days, that land sat in East Bridgewater. In 1875, as part of the great reshuffling of the former Old Abington, the residents of that small section of town seceded from East Bridgewater to join the people of South Abington in a new town: Whitman.

So Ruth and Kenneth opened their restaurant and ran it for the next thirty-seven years, giving it the fictitious date of 1709 and equally fictitious moniker as a "toll house." As longtime Abington historian Martha Campbell remembered:

> They opened, first, in the depths of the 1929 depression, and soon became known as the place to get a fine, full-course meal, elegantly served, all for $1. People managed to find the dollars, and they began flocking here in droves. The dining room, then, was only the front room of the little Cape Cod cottage. The establishment had to grow along with the clientele.

Although the restaurant was not really a toll house, it was a good gimmick. *Courtesy of Historical Society of Old Abington.*

Finally, it encompassed the well-known circular "garden room," built around a great tree trunk. The garden room windows looked out on the well-groomed real garden, which was at perfection at every season.

The Wakefields, driven by Ruth's sharp eye for style, sought artifacts from around the world, with some of their ornamental glassware being photographed for the *Woman's Day Dictionary of Sandwich Glass* in 1963. "The service was elegant, the appointments superb, with real linen and silver, and handsome place plates echoing the table decorations. A large hook was provided under each table corner for hanging milady's purse out of the way," remembered Campbell.

Keeping the place looking that way was a chore, said the former waitress. Every napkin had to be folded perfectly. The entire waitstaff had to work without paper, committing orders to memory. In order to keep up appearances, Ruth trained her waiters and waitresses to never shout out at the tables, "OK, who had the steak?!"

Amidst all of this finery, Ruth Wakefield unwittingly made one of the greatest single contributions to American dessert cuisine. One night in 1937, having run out of baker's chocolate and desirous of finishing a batch of cookies for the restaurant's patrons, she dropped pieces of Nestle's semisweet chocolate into the bowl, figuring they would melt. When she pulled the cookies out of the oven, she discovered that they hadn't and, even more surprisingly, that folks loved the cookies as they were. She had mistakenly invented the chocolate chip cookie, although she called it the "Toll House Crunch Cookie."

Sales soared, and Ruth made a deal with Andrew Nestle himself: the right to print the recipe on packages of Nestle chocolate (which Nestle started to market in morsel form, specifically for cookies) for a free lifetime supply of the chocolate. Chocolate chip cookies became one of America's favorite desserts—but not everybody had access to them. Our anonymous waitress remembered how at the end of each night, Ruth would bag up the extra cookies and order them thrown out. The waitstaff was not allowed to snack on them, whatsoever. One night, though, they took their chance, and ended up paying the price. The waitress recalled:

> *We knew that Ruth wouldn't be there, so we all put in our order at the end of the evening. We wanted a private place in which to eat them after the restaurant closed, and since Ruth wasn't there, we used her office. Well, guess who walked in. She never said a word. She just looked at what each of us was eating, made eye contact with each of us individually, and walked out. The next week, the exact cost of our desserts was taken out of our paychecks.*

The Wakefields ran the Toll House Inn until 1967. It operated for four more years under new owners until 1971, at which point it closed for good. It burned down in 1984 and today the site is occupied by a Wendy's and a Walgreens. Martha Campbell summed up the story of the Wakefields and their Toll House Inn: "Nobody ever really worried about the imaginative date and name for this restaurant. Everybody knew that it was just good promotional technique, and everybody who ever ate there will always remember the days of the Wakefields, which were both 'good' and, now, 'old.'"

1941: Fire at Ocean Bluff

While every South Shore fire company has a story to tell about the biggest blaze its crews ever had to battle, no local department can claim to have faced a conflagration on their own turf like the inferno that struck the Ocean Bluff area of Marshfield at 1:40 p.m., Monday, April 21, 1941. It all started with a small, briefly and seemingly completely controllable fire on the corner of Plymouth Avenue and Ocean Street—until prevailing thirty-mile-per-hour winds upped the ante.

Much stood to be lost. While once a place of bucolic agrarian scenery, with cattle grazing on wide, rambling fields lined by farmer-built stone walls, Ocean Bluff had by the end of the nineteenth century become a beloved summer retreat to many annually returning families. Easy access to the ocean and its many salubrious offerings—saltwater bathing, fresh ocean breezes and even the chance to snag a fish or two for a meal fresh from the heart of nature—attracted leisure seekers and, ultimately, land speculators and developers. By 1941, Ocean Bluff, former farmland, had become one of the most tightly congested villages of any South Shore town.

The fire, though, cared naught for history. It spread quickly from the open marshland where it started at Fieldston to the grid-like streets of Ocean Bluff, indiscriminately igniting house after house. With the wind at its back, the blaze marched unabated to the south, reaching Samoset Street. For four hours, the flames leapt skyward, shattering the seaside dreams of hundreds of summer residents. Smoke climbed into the sky until it became visible in Provincetown to the east and as far to the south as Nantucket Island. Fire companies from the surrounding area roused themselves into action and headed for the scene as the fire spread across the grasses left brittle by an unseasonable stretch of dry spring weather.

Only with the setting of the sun came the crucial abatement of the winds. At 5:30 p.m., the firefighters, many of them volunteers, wrestled the flames into submission, but the damage had been done. Where once summer carousers walked gaily and carefree through the streets now lay the remains of an entire Marshfield village. "The devastation was total," stated Cynthia Krusell and Betty Magoun Bates in *Marshfield: A Town of Villages*. "Two hotels, the post office, the Casino, the church, twelve stores, 446 houses and cottages, and 96 garages." St. Ann's church, symbolic of the growth of the Irish Catholic population in the village, withstood the worst the fire had to offer, ultimately losing everything but its walls. Yet the fire did not cause the parish to shut down, by any means; the current St. Ann's by the Sea was constructed in 1957.

Ocean Bluff, though, as thousands had known it, was no more.

In the days that followed, summer residents—many of whom lived in nearby Abington and whose seasonal presence gave the area its nickname, Abington Village—arrived to sift through the ruins to see if anything but their memories survived the blaze. Instead, they found a wasteland. Cars had burned, as had hotels. Even the firetrucks themselves had become victims to the inferno they had fought to control.

Marshfield's year-round and summer residents alike, though, could pull two unbelievable bright spots out of the otherwise all-pervading gloom. While thirty people were left homeless by the firestorm, not a single life had been lost, mostly due to the fact that the summer crowd had not yet arrived for the season. Second, stated Krusell and Bates, while "burned hoses and fire engines littered the street. The Ocean Bluff fire station on Massassoit Avenue, however, survived the fire."

Fire Chief Silas S. Wright felt the entire situation could have been avoided, telling the *Quincy Patriot Ledger* the next day that if the town fathers had allowed their usual annual appropriation for proscribed burning of the marsh grass, the fire might never have started in the first place. Among those buildings lost was a store owned by the chief.

In an act of pure faith, the town of Marshfield moved quickly to rebuild. In 1941, the United States was still mired in the last days of the Great Depression, and in April, it stood just more than half a year away from entry into World War II. In the end, the fire put many Marshfield residents back to work, cleaning up the wreckage and building new streets. Surveying the desolation of the burned-over wasteland, one could not help but think that better days had to be ahead for Ocean Bluff.

1957: *Mayflower II*

I t was a great plan.

Nobody alive had ever seen the original *Mayflower*. In fact, today's most persistent rumors claim its remains are now tucked into the architecture of a seventeenth-century barn somewhere in England. Furthermore, nobody had ever seen any plans for the construction of the original ship, nor had even any crude drawings been left behind. Not only had no one ever seen *Mayflower*, no one even knew what it looked like.

But it was still a great plan.

Warwick Charlton, described by his widow, Melinda, in 2007 as "not a sailor, but a writer, author, journalist, playwright, publicist, entrepreneur, and soldier," always felt that the British people never fully appreciated what the Americans accomplished for them in World War II. So in August 1954, he proposed a transatlantic gift. "Why he hit on a replica *Mayflower* I have no idea," said Melinda.

Charlton started to chase down his dream. He secured financial backing and contacted new friends across the sea, hoping to find a final home for his creation. A fledgling museum, just getting started in Plymouth, Massachusetts, agreed to take the replica vessel when it reached the United States. It even conceived of a permanent dry berth along the Eel River for a static display. *Mayflower II*, if it ever came to reality, would have a home in the town that made *Mayflower* famous.

Even more serendipitously, though, Plimoth Plantation had already in 1951 commissioned naval architect William Baker of Hingham to devise plans

More than a half-century since its arrival on the Plymouth waterfront, the *Mayflower II* is still a popular attraction. *Courtesy of the author.*

for a replica *Mayflower* for its own planned exhibit. With Charlton's fast-moving publicist's tongue (and inherent fundraising ability) and Baker's plans, *Mayflower II* took steps closer from abstract notion to concrete actuality. The Upham shipyard in Brixham, Devonshire, England, agreed to take on the challenge of its construction, and a crew, led by the famed

In 2007, the *Mayflower II* sailed on its fiftieth anniversary, thanks to volunteers like this one. *Courtesy of the author.*

Captain Allan Villiers, came together for the promised-to-be dramatic sail across the Atlantic.

As the ship prepared to sail, Charlton tuned up the media hype. Melinda later said that *Mayflower II* "sailed across the ocean on gales of publicity." The two nations, still healing from the pain, heartache and heavy losses of World War II, found a common spectacle to rally around. The ship slid down the ways and into Brixham Harbor on September 22, 1956. On April 20, 1957, it set sail for America, choosing a southerly route across the sea.

"As for myself," Villiers wrote in *National Geographic* ("How We Sailed *Mayflower II* to America," Volume 112, No. 5), "I was thrilled to be her master, doing my best to sail her to Plymouth, Massachusetts, where she belonged. But I'd have been a little more thrilled had the wind blown better." Following ancient traditions, as if scripted directly from a seventeenth-century ship's log, *Mayflower II* found the Atlantic's notorious doldrums and drifted lazily for days on end. "I began to wonder whether we would ever come in at all," he wrote.

However, then as also as in days of yore, the weather turned. On June 8, after more than six listless weeks at sea, a gale blew up that tested the

Looking Back at South Shore History

mettle of the crew off Bermuda. Hardened sailors one and all, save for the cabin boys, one each from England and the United States (young Joe Meany of Waltham had earned the spot through the Boys' Club of America), the crew fought through bravely, tending to the sails and lines with professional deftness. Such an occurrence reflected Warwick Charlton's greatest fears. "He had some rather dark thoughts about the voyage," said Melinda, "and hoped nobody could read his thoughts." The ship and the crew came through, literally, with colors flying.

On June 11, *Mayflower II* passed the Nantucket Lightship, touching down at Provincetown the following day, exactly as the original vessel had in 1620. On June 13, 1957, *Mayflower II* arrived in Plymouth Harbor, fifty-five days after setting sail in England. Thousands cheered from the shore.

Warwick Charlton was not done. In 1997, at a three-day celebration for the fortieth anniversary of the sail in Plymouth, England, he envisioned his next big *Mayflower II* publicity stunt. "For the fiftieth anniversary," said Melinda, "his vowed intention was to kidnap the ship, sail it into England, keep it in the harbor over winter and give it back in spring." Sadly, Charlton never saw the fiftieth anniversary, passing away in 2002 at age eighty-four. His legacy, still afloat, still a major tourist attraction for the region and still occasionally sailing the waters off Plymouth, lives on.

About the Author

J ohn Galluzzo is the author of more than thirty-five books on the history
and nature of Massachusetts and the northeast, and the U.S. Coast Guard
on a national scale. He writes for the *Hull Times, Scituate Mariner* and *South
Shore Living* on a regular basis, devoting his full-time energies to the South
Shore Natural Science Center, where he is director of education. He grew
up in Hull and has lived in Hingham, Scituate, Weymouth and Hanover,
and although he travels all over the country as a writer and lecturer, he never
envisions leaving the South Shore of Massachusetts.